高等职业教育"十二五"规划教材　高等职业英语数字教材研究项目

# Contemporary Business English Listening and Speaking Course

# 当代商务英语听说教程 2

第 2 版　学生用书

总 主 编　何兆熊
本册主编　姜荷梅　何光明
编　者　姜荷梅　何光明　金　阳　孙　怡　王虹慧

华东师范大学出版社
·上海·

图书在版编目(CIP)数据

当代商务英语听说教程学生用书.2/姜荷梅,荷光明主编.—2版.—上海:华东师范大学出版社,2014.7
ISBN 978-7-5675-2386-9

Ⅰ.①当… Ⅱ.①姜…②何… Ⅲ.①商务-英语-听说教学-高等学校-教材 Ⅳ.①H319.9

中国版本图书馆 CIP 数据核字(2014)第 172388 号

高等职业教育"十二五"规划教材　高等职业英语数字化教材研究项目
## 当代商务英语听说教程学生用书2(第二版)

总 主 编　何兆熊
本册主编　姜荷梅　何光明
责任编辑　李恒平
责任校对　王秀娥
封面设计　孔薇薇

出版发行　华东师范大学出版社
社　　址　上海市中山北路3663号 邮编 200062
网　　址　www.ecnupress.com.cn
电　　话　021-60821666　行政传真 021-62572105
客服电话　021-62865537　门市(邮购)电话 021-62869887
地　　址　上海市中山北路3663号华东师范大学校内先锋路口
网　　店　http://hdsdcbs.tmall.com

印 刷 者　昆山市亭林印刷有限责任公司
开　　本　787毫米×1092毫米　1/16
印　　张　14.75
字　　数　286千字
版　　次　2014年8月第2版
印　　次　2023年7月第7次
书　　号　ISBN 978-7-5675-2386-9/H·714
定　　价　38.60元(含盘)

出版人　王　焰

(如发现本版图书有印订质量问题,请寄回本社客服中心调换或电话 021-62865537 联系)

# 编者说明

《当代商务英语听说教程》第一至四册为基础阶段听说教材,供高职高专商务英语专业或应用英语专业学生使用,也可供程度相当的自学者使用。

英语语言基础在商务英语教学中的重要地位和作用是显而易见的。在经济全球化浪潮的冲击下,各种涉外工作对外语人才特别是商务英语人才的要求越来越高。这也对教学和教材编写提出了更高的要求。由于高职高专商务英语教学研究起步较晚等多方面原因,出现了相关教材跟不上形势的情况,商务英语听说优秀教材更是极为匮乏。针对这些状况,我们编写本系列教材,希望能对解决这些问题做出我们微薄的贡献。

本教程以高等职业技术学院、独立本科院校商务英语专业学生入学水平的中等程度为起点,即在学习本教程之前,学生已掌握基本的英语语音和语法知识,能认知1900个左右的英语单词(掌握其中1 200个),并在听、说、读、写等方面受过初步训练。在学完本教程后,力争做到:中上等水平的学生可以流畅地在工作中使用英语进行沟通,能够从事一般商务英语工作;中等水平的学生基本可以用英语进行交流和沟通,能够从事使用英语的相关商务工作。

本教程第二册围绕与客户直接进行英语沟通为主题,挑选与客户沟通最常见的话题,如:与客户预约、接待客户、产品介绍、初步商务洽谈、价格磋商、宴请客户、签约、跟单等。目的是希望学习者通过学习本书,能够和客户用英语就工作内容进行沟通。本册丰富的话题进一步彰显商务英语的本质特点——实用性,并为步入商界打下坚实的基础。

**本书各单元由如下部分组成:**

Part 1　Practical Listening and Speaking(实用听说)
　　Word study
　　Functional listening
　　Language check
　　Controlled practice
　　Business culture
Part 2　Business Speaking(商务口语)
　　Pair work
　　Role play
Part 3　Listening Practice(听力技能训练)
　　Listening focus
　　Dictation

Conversations

Passage

Part 4　Fun Listening(轻松一刻)

**本书各部分内容有如下特点：**
Part 1　Practical Listening and Speaking(实用听说)
根据最新的语言教学研究成果，本部分将听说结合在一起训练，旨在帮助学生实现从"听：输入——(通过模仿进而)内化——输出：说"的有效循环。通过听说结合训练，让学生在掌握各种听力技能的同时，学习并掌握常见的商务英语词汇和功能句型以及相关的商务沟通技巧和文化差异。本部分可为实际商务沟通打下扎实的基础，因而实用性和针对性较强。

1) **Word study**
- 听力训练：本部分的词汇和句子配有录音，可以作为听力训练的材料，目的主要是操练重点词汇的听写。
- 口语训练：在听之前，可让学生朗读或口头完成词汇填空。
- 实用性与交际性：所有词汇皆为常见、实用商务词汇，按照单元话题进行挑选，听力和口语都选自实际情景练习，学生学习后可以直接在真实场景情况下使用。
- 特色与创新：大部分同类教材只是简单将词汇罗列出来，本书根据商务语境，有针对性的提供相关词汇，让学习者真正全面地掌握实用商务新词汇。

2) **Functional listening**
- 听力训练：第二册为提高级，本部分听力的练习形式主要选用填空题和正误题。学生在操练时，会觉得轻松一些，从而提高学习兴趣，增强信心。
- 口语训练：这部分的听力材料也可以用作口语材料。
- 实用性：这部分听力练习皆按照单元话题及常见表达功能进行编写，在参考许多商务英语教材的基础上注意提炼最适合学生的表达。
- 交际性：这部分的听力材料也可以用作口语材料。教师和学生之间以及学生与学生之间都可以进行充分的交流。
- 特色与创新：这部分按照常见商务话题及常见功能表达进行编排，故更具系统性、实用性，教学目标明确。

3) **Language check**
- 听力训练：该部分听力训练重点在于功能句型的听写，为口语打基础。
- 口语训练：将功能分解成小话题进行操练，逐个击破、分项掌握，从而让学生更好地记住功能表达，自如地应用功能表达。
- 实用性与交际性：该部分为第二部分听力(Functional listening)的细分，内容切合实用。同时，该部分材料完全适合做口语材料。
- 特色与创新：与国际接轨，国外许多优秀教材都采取了这种听说练习形式。

4) **Controlled practice**
- 听力训练：该部分听力材料仍然围绕单元话题展开，但具体细节和第二部分听力

(Functional listening)有差别,依然是实用的听力材料。
- ◇ 口语训练:学生可以按照提示进行互动操练,进一步掌握功能句型,增强口语表达能力。
- ➢ 实用性:所选材料来自(或充分模拟)真实商务场景。
- ➢ 交际性:该部分材料完全适合做口语材料,有利于调动课堂气氛。
- ➢ 特色与创新:该种练习形式在国内同类教材应用不多,而国外商务英语教材正逐渐使用。

5) **Business culture**
- ◇ 听力训练:练习形式采取了填空题和正误题,难度适合学生认知水平。
- ◇ 口语训练:在听之前,可以通过回答问题的形式展开口语训练。
- ➢ 实用性:所选内容为商务文化及沟通技巧,皆为编者多年来外企商务英语培训内容的精华。
- ➢ 交际性:这部分内容以交际沟通技巧和文化差异为主,并配有口语练习。
- ➢ 特色与创新:内容涉及全面,针对性与实用性强。这部分内容是本书的一大亮点。

### Part 2　Business Speaking(商务口语)

本部分围绕单元商务话题展开口语训练,从有控制的训练开始,过渡到半开放性的训练,最后达到自由的交流与沟通。练习形式有对话、问题、角色表演、小组讨论等。不同级别练习的难度不同,皆由浅入深、循序渐进。所有材料扣紧真实商务题材,让学生能尽可能模拟真实商务场景,最终达到商务沟通无障碍。

1) **Pair work**
- ◇ 口语训练:采取搭档操练形式,进一步巩固功能句型。
- ➢ 实用性:选材围绕话题,突出功能表达。
- ➢ 交际性:该部分操练形式为控制型和半开放性的训练,互动性和交际性强。
- ➢ 特色与创新:内容充实、针对强、实用。

2) **Role play**
- ◇ 口语训练:采取角色表演形式,可两人或多个人参与。提供的材料多为图片和表格,直观易懂。
- ➢ 实用性:所选内容来自(或模拟)真实商务场景,学生不仅能提高英语沟通技能还可以丰富商务知识,具有很强的实用性。
- ➢ 交际性:该部分操练形式为半开放性的训练和自由交际,互动性和交际性很强。
- ➢ 特色与创新:这部分内容图文并茂,学生学得愉快。

### Part 3　Listening Practice(听力技能训练)

相对于第一部分的听力,本部分为听力微技能训练,更为侧重听力技能的提高。所选材料大多围绕商务话题,练习形式丰富多样。不仅便于学生快速提高听力水平,同时也为学生参加各种商务英语考试(如:BEC、BULATS、TOEIC 等)做好充分准备。

### Part 4　Fun Listening(轻松一刻)

本部分为轻松的听力活动,主要选取歌曲、电影录音片断,辅以绕口令、笑话、幽默等内容。为学生创造轻松的听说氛围,提高学习的趣味性。

本书使用说明：

Part 1    Practical Listening and Speaking(实用听说)

Word study

约占10分钟。教师可以在前一节课布置给学生，让学生预习生词。若学生口语基础较好的话，可让学生进行搭档完成词汇填空，然后再听；反之，则可以直接进入听力训练，跳过口语练习。

Functional listening

约占10~15分钟。教师可以根据上课时间灵活使用该部分内容。若教师将听说结合起来操练，则这部分可以用作角色扮演的材料。

Language check

约占10分钟。教师可以根据学生的水平灵活使用该部分内容。若学生口语基础较好的话，则可以缩短操练时间；反之，则操练时间可以长些。最终目的是能让学生记住并能灵活应用这些功能表达。

Controlled practice

约占10分钟。教师可以根据授课时间和学生水平灵活使用。

Business culture

约占10分钟。教师可以布置学生预习本部分内容。

Part 2    Business Speaking(商务口语)

Pair work

约占15分钟。这部分的两人对话是针对第一部分听说结合的功能和情景设计的，应提醒学生在交流中多使用和操练已学的句型。

Role play

约占15~20分钟。这部分内容教师可以让学生上台表演。表演活动可以活跃课堂气氛，激发学生学习兴趣，鼓励学生大胆开口说。教师应注意提醒学生用英语交流或表达。

Part 3    Listening Practice(听力训练)：

约占30分钟或作课后练习。教师可以作为听力训练在课堂上完成。也可以布置学生课后完成本部分内容。

Part 4    Fun Listening(轻松一刻)

约占5分钟。这部分内容教师可以让学生课后温习。

为了方便教师使用，本教程配备了较为详尽的教师用书。每单元的教师用书由两部分组成：第一部分是教学建议；第二部分是录音材料和Key to exercises，在必要之处我们对所给答案作了简单的解释。我们的意图是把教师用书变成一本十分实用、使用方便的教学参考书。

本教程第一至四册由姜荷梅老师与何光明老师合作编写。本册中何光明老师编写每单元第一二部分，姜荷梅老师负责每单元第三四部分，其余部分由李恒平老师负责。美籍商务英语教学专家John Parker审定教程所有英文。参加本教程第二册编写工作的有姜荷梅、何光明、王虹惠、孙怡、金阳、李恒平等教师。

　　本教程在编写过程中得到常玉田教授（对外经济贸易大学）、邹为诚教授（华东师范大学）、陈洁教授（上海对外贸易学院商务英语学院）、王大伟教授（上海海事大学）、张武保副教授与欧阳护华教授（广东外语外贸大学商务英语学院）、井升华教授（商务英语专家）和刘法公教授（浙江工商大学）等多位英语界和商务英语教学界专家的支持，在此一并对他们表示衷心的感谢。

何兆熊

2007年12月

　　本书第一版得到广大师生的喜爱和欢迎，根据教师的使用意见，本次修订仍保留了原有的框架与设计，仅对文字做了修订和补充，并增、删了少量图片，以期完善。

编　者

2014年6月

# Acknowledgement

We are extremely grateful to the authors and publishing houses for all the materials chosen as content in this textbook. We hope that the request for permission to use the related resources for teaching purposes will receive kind and generous consideration.

Every effort has been made to contact copyright holders before publication. However, in some cases this has been impossible. If contacted, the publisher will ensure that full credit is given at the earliest opportunity.

# Bookmap

| Units | Contents | Functional listening | Business culture | Listening strategies |
|---|---|---|---|---|
| Unit 1 | *Could I send you our catalogue* | Getting past the secretary on the phone<br>Answering clients' questions on the phone | Understanding telephone manners | Identifying some important abbreviations<br>Answering clients' questions on the phone<br>Taking telephone messages |
| Unit 2 | *When would be good for you* | Making an appointment<br>Changing an appointment | Understanding time cultures | Understanding airport announcements |
| Unit 3 | *Where would you like to stay* | Describing hotels<br>Booking hotels for clients | Understanding Chinese modesty culture | Understanding directions and positions<br>Making a reservation |
| Unit 4 | *Welcome to our company* | Meeting a client at the airport<br>Receiving a client at the office | Knowing eight questions you should not ask | Identifying geographical locations<br>Introducing a company |
| Unit 5 | *What would you like for the starter* | Dining in a Western restaurant<br>Making, accepting and declining invitations | Understanding Western table manners | Understanding lines, angles and shapes |
| Unit 6 | *This is our new showroom* | Describing a product in the showroom<br>Explaining the catalogue | Understanding personal space | Understanding public signs |
| Unit 7 | *Let me tell you more about our product* | Making a sales presentation<br>Demonstrating a product | Learning three *Ps* for presentations | Making a sales presentation<br>Understanding tips for a successful presentation |
| Unit 8 | *Would you like to visit our factory* | Showing someone around the factory and answering questions<br>Describing the production process | Opening and ending the business talk | Knowing about production process<br>Understanding three main types of production process<br>Understanding five steps for opening and ending a first business talk |

| Units | Contents | Functional listening | Business culture | Listening strategies |
|---|---|---|---|---|
| Unit 9 | This is our lowest price | Negotiating prices and discounts<br>Negotiating terms of payment | Developing relationships first or doing business first | Following instructions while listening<br>Applying skills of a good salesperson |
| Unit 10 | What would you like to order | Placing an order on the phone<br>Tracking an order on the phone | Improving your listening on the phone | Guessing meanings while listening<br>Understanding how to place an order |
| Unit 11 | We can make the delivery in June | Talking about delivery time<br>Talking about shipment | Understanding gifting culture | Listening for key words<br>Discussing delivery time |
| Unit 12 | What about packing and insurance | Talking about packing<br>Talking about insurance | Understanding the Chinese offer & decline culture | Listening for specific details<br>Understanding people talking about packing<br>Understanding people talking about insurance<br>Understanding a brief introduction of insurance |
| Unit 13 | Shall we sign the contract | Signing a contract<br>Toasting at a farewell dinner | Learning tips for making a toast | Listening for the main idea<br>Understanding people talking about a contract<br>Understanding what a contract is |
| Unit 14 | When can you make the payment | Chasing payment in a polite way<br>Chasing payment in a serious way | Learning tips for collecting money on time | Predicting while listening<br>Understanding how to chase overdue payments |
| Unit 15 | I'm sorry to hear that | Making a complaint<br>Dealing with a complaint | Learning tips for making and dealing with complaints | Taking notes while listening |
| Unit 16 | How was the last order | Calling a previous client<br>Describing the sales trend | Learning 5 tips for a successful sales call | Summarizing while listening<br>Learning lessons from an ineffective sales call |

# Contents

Unit 1  Could I send you our catalogue ················· 1

Unit 2  When would be good for you ················· 13

Unit 3  Where would you like to stay ················· 25

Unit 4  Welcome to our company ················· 41

Unit 5  What would you like for the starter ················· 55

Unit 6  This is our new showroom ················· 71

Unit 7  Let me tell you more about our product ················· 84

Unit 8  Would you like to visit our factory ················· 96

Unit 9  This is our lowest price ················· 110

Unit 10  What would you like to order ················· 124

Unit 11  We can make delivery in June ················· 137

Unit 12  What about packing and insurance ················· 149

Unit 13  Shall we sign the contract ················· 162

Unit 14  When can you make the payment ················· 174

Unit 15  I'm sorry to hear that ················· 188

Unit 16  How was the last order ················· 202

Appendix ················· 215

# Unit 1  Could I send you our catalogue

## Unit Goals

◇ Getting past the secretary on the phone
◇ Answering clients' questions on the phone
◇ Understanding telephone manners
◇ Identifying some important abbreviations
◇ Taking telephone messages

## Part 1  Practical Listening & Speaking

### A  Word study

Work with your partner to fill in the blanks using the words on the left. Listen and check your answers, and then follow the recording.

| office stationery |
| market leader |
| Personal Assistant |
| contact |
| latest model |
| retail price |
| discount |
| from stock |
| out of stock |

(1) Your _____ _____ is too high. How about $ 500 per machine?

(2) If we buy 40 machines, how large is your _____?

(3) We can't supply _____ _____ at the moment.

(4) Do you have a 7-day _____ _____? I mean, if the goods are poor in quality, can we return them to you within 7 days?

(5) The _____ _____ is very important. We need to have your people look at our machines in time if they are broken-down.

(6) The goods are _____ _____ _____ at the moment.

(7) I'm afraid your _____ _____ is too short. Can you make it 3 years?

(8) Please feel free to _____ me anytime.

(9) Could you _____ the goods to us as soon as possible? We can't wait.

1

| deliver |
| warranty period |
| on-site maintenance |
| money-back guarantee |

(10) We are short of _____ _____. Can we buy some now?
(11) I work as the _____ _____ to Mr. Jackson, our General Manager.
(12) We are a _____ _____ in the office furniture business.
(13) This is our _____ _____. It's very popular with our customers.

## B Functional listening

*Task One (Getting past the secretary on the phone)*: Listen to the recording and fill in the blanks.

Joy: Good morning. THT Corporation.
Don: Good morning. This is Don Barry calling from PLP Office Stationery. (1) _____ Purchasing Manager, please?
Joy: Could I ask what it's about?
Don: (2) _____ the Purchasing Manager about the possibility of providing our office stationery for you. We are a market leader in this field.
Joy: Yes, I see. He is not available just now.
Don: Could you (3) _____?
Joy: He's very busy for the next few days.
Don: Would you mind asking him to call me back?
Joy: Sorry. I don't think I could do that. He's very busy right now.
Don: Do you think I could speak to someone else?
Joy: (4) _____. I can deal with his calls.
Don: Is it all right if I call him tomorrow?
Joy: I'm sorry he won't be free tomorrow. May I suggest that you (5) _____ and then we'll contact you?
Don: Yes, that's very kind of you. I have your address.
Joy: Right, Mr. Barry. We look forward to hearing from you.
Don: Thank you. Goodbye.
Joy: Bye.

**Task Two** (*Answering clients' questions on the phone*): Listen to the telephone conversation and complete the following notes using one or two words from the recording.

(1) The retail price of Model 679 is _____.

(2) The man's company can supply the goods _____.

(3) The man's company can deliver the goods to the woman's company within _____ _____.

(4) The warranty period of this model is _____ _____. The man's company can also provide _____ maintenance service.

## ❸ Language check

Work with your partner to complete the following conversations, and then listen and check your answers.

*Task One: Getting past the secretary on the phone*

*Introducing yourself and asking to speak to somebody*

M: This is John Johnson calling from PRK. Could I speak to the Finance Manager, please?

F: Could I ask (1) _____ it's about?

*Stating the purpose*

M: I'd like to speak to the Finance Manager about the possibility of (2) _____ our office furniture for you. We are a market leader in this field.

F: OK, I see. He is not available just now.

*Asking when you can get hold of him*

M: (3) _____ _____ tell me when I can reach him?

F: He's very busy for the next few days.

*Asking him to call you back*

M: (4) _____ _____ _____ asking him to call me back?

F: Sorry. I don't think I could do that. He's very busy.

*Asking to speak to someone else*

M: Do (5) _____ _____ I could speak to someone else?

F: I'm afraid not. I can deal with his calls.

*Asking to call in the near future*

M: Is (6) _____ _____ if I call him tomorrow?
F: I'm afraid you can't. He's really busy these days.

*Asking to send your catalogue*

M: Could I send you our catalogue?
F: OK.

**Task Two: Answering clients' questions on the phone**

*Answering questions about prices and discounts*

M: How (1) _____ does it cost?
F: Our retail price is RMB 1,300.
M: If we buy 30, what's your (2) _____ _____?
F: We can allow you a 25% discount.

*Answering questions about the stock and delivery*

M: Can you (3) _____ it _____ stock?
F: I'm sorry. It's out of stock now.
M: Then when can you make (4) _____ _____?
F: It will take one month to produce the product. We can deliver the goods to you in 45 days.

*Answering questions about the warranty period and other guarantee*

M: What's your (5) _____ _____?
F: Our warranty period is 6 months.
M: Do you have a 7-day (6) _____ guarantee?
F: Sorry. I'm afraid we don't have that guarantee.

*Answering questions about maintenance service*

M: Do you provide (7) _____ maintenance service?
F: Yes, we provide on-site maintenance service free of charge within the (8) _____ _____. Our engineers can arrive at your company within 24 hours after your call.

## D Controlled practice

You are a buyer. Your partner is a seller. Work with him or her to make a dialogue based on the following flow chart. Listen to the recording of a model answer, and then follow it.

Unit 1

| YOU | YOUR PARTNER |
|---|---|
| Ask for the retail price. | Offer $542. |
| Ask for a discount. | Say the discount depends on the size of order. |
| Ask for the largest discount on 10,000 units. | Offer 25%. |
| Ask about the delivery date. | Say 60 days. |
| Ask about the warranty period. | Say 6 months. |

## E Business culture

Work with your partner to answer the following questions. Then listen to Justin Comfort and Anne Heaton talk about their telephoning experiences in China, and fill in the blanks.

(1) What would you do if your mobile phone rang in your meeting with a client?

(2) When you are having an important meeting, do you think it is necessary to switch off your mobile phone or put it to vibration(震动)?

(3) Have you ever received a wrong call? How did you handle it? If you dial a wrong number, what will you say to the called party?

*Telephoning Manners*

*Justin Comfort:* "I was having a one-to-one _____ with Mr. Chong Ping, one of my Chinese clients. When we were having a discussion, Mr. Chong's mobile phone rang. He stood up and had a talk (2) _____ _____ _____, leaving me alone. After his phone call, he didn't say anything, and we (3) _____ our discussion. However, after a short while, Mr. Chong's cell phone rang again. This time, I said (4) _____, 'Could we finish our business first?' Mr. Chong could not but (5) _____ his head, saying yes. Just before the end of the talk, Mr. Chong's (6) _____ came in, telling him that there was an important phone call for him. I was (7) _____."

*Anne Heaton:* "One day, when I was answering a phone call, I heard a loud voice on the other end (8) _____, 'Wei? Wei?' Since the people who (9) _____ call me usually say, 'Hello?' I knew that this caller had dialed a wrong number. I was hesitant(犹豫的) in (10) _____ to the voice, (11) _____ the caller to speak louder and stronger. 'Dui bu qi, ni da cuo le. (I'm afraid you have dialed the wrong number.)' I finally said, hoping he would (12) _____ _____. Soon, he was asking me who I was, my phone number, job and (13) _____ salary. I couldn't believe he was asking so many (14) _____ questions. Even worse, I kept on answering each question. I must have (15) _____ that if I answered just one more question, he would stop asking. But with each question answered, he (16) _____ asking questions. 'Da cuo le! (Wrong number)' Finally I shouted back and hung up."

# Part 2  Business Speaking

## A Pair work

*Task One:* Work with your partner to match the sentences on the left with the similar sentences on the right. Then Student A says the sentences on the left, and Student B should try to respond with similar sentences without looking at the book. After the practice, change roles.

(1) I'm afraid the goods are out of stock.
(2) He is not available just now.
(3) Would you mind asking him to call me back?
(4) Is it OK if I call him tomorrow?
(5) May I suggest that you send us your catalogue first?
(6) What's your largest discount?
(7) How fast can you deliver the goods to us?
(8) Can you supply from stock?
(9) How long is your warranty period?

A. Could you ask him to call me back?
B. Is it all right if I call him tomorrow?
C. Could you send us your catalogue first?
D. I'm afraid we can't supply from stock.
E. How large is your discount?
F. He is busy at the moment.
G. What's your warranty period?
H. When can you make the delivery?
I. Do you have the goods in stock?

*Task Two:* Choose the most appropriate response by ticking A, B or C. Then practice the dialogues.

(1) Can I take a message?

A. I'd like to leave a message.
B. Yes, could you ask him to call me back?
C. Ask him to give me a ring.

(2) The reason I called is we're having some problems with your product.

A. I don't believe it.
B. Really? That surprises me.
C. I don't mind.

(3) So that's fixed — Friday at 11 o'clock.

A. I'm afraid that's out of the question.
B. Right, I look forward to seeing you then.
C. Goodbye.

## B Role play

*Task One:* Role-play a telephone conversation according to the following situations. After the practice, change roles.

*Information for you*
Use your own name.

You work in the Sales Department of ABC Computing. It is your job to deal with customer enquiries. Answer the phone and note down the caller's name and address and what information he or she wants.

*Information for your partner*
This is your business card.

```
KLA
SYSTEMS
John Martin


PO Box 45, Coral Gables, RE43435
```

You want some information about the Vari-X line. Phone ABC Computing and ask them to send you a brochure.

*Task Two:* When you take a message, you can't write down the whole sentence. That means you can only take notes. For example, when you hear "You can phone me anytime but I won't be here tomorrow afternoon", you may write "Phone before 12 tomorrow", Your partner reads the following sentences, and you take notes. Then change roles and compare your notes with the reference answer.

| | |
|---|---|
| (1) I'd like you to send me a catalogue. If you can fax this, that would be fine. | Send catalogue by fax. |
| (2) Could you get someone to pick me up at the airport? My plane gets in at half past ten. | Pick up at airport at 10:30. |
| (3) Can you book a hotel room for me from July 7 to 12, if possible at the Holiday Inn? | Book hotel from July 7-12, Holiday Inn. |
| (4) For your information, the price of your hotel room includes a breakfast. | Price includes breakfast. |
| (5) Can you fax me a copy of the agreement as soon as possible, please? | Fax agreement ASAP. |
| (6) Could you please also send me any information you have on the meeting we had in July? | Send information on meeting in July. |
| (7) My phone number is 467-2455667, and the extension number is 233. | Call 467-2455667-233. |

## Part 3　Listening Practice

### A　Listening focus

**Abbreviations**

*Task One:* You will hear the names of abbreviations of world-famous companies. Listen carefully and write down the full names next to the abbreviations.

(1) COCA-COLA _____
(2) MICROSOFT _____
(3) IBM _____
(4) GE _____
(5) INTEL _____
(6) NOKIA _____

*Task Two:* You will hear 20 abbreviations from business English. Listen carefully and write them down in the left column. Then match them with the phrases in the right column.

Unit 1

| Abbreviations | Phrases |
|---|---|
| ( J ) (1) _____ | A. as soon as possible |
| ( B ) (2) _____ | B. with reference to, regarding |
| ( O ) (3) _____ | C. delivery order |
| ( C ) (4) _____ | D. enclosure(s) |
| ( S ) (5) _____ | E. Information Technology |
| ( D ) (6) _____ | F. value added tax |
| ( R ) (7) _____ | G. Gross Domestic Product |
| ( L ) (8) _____ | H. Master of Business Administration |
| ( T ) (9) _____ | I. Personal Digital Assistant |
| ( A ) (10) _____ | J. Corporation |
| ( P ) (11) _____ | K. Research and Design |
| ( G ) (12) _____ | L. Central Process Unit |
| ( Q ) (13) _____ | M. Multimedia Messaging Service |
| ( N ) (14) _____ | N. International Standardization Organization |
| ( E ) (15) _____ | O. balance sheet |
| ( H ) (16) _____ | P. limited |
| ( I ) (17) _____ | Q. Internet Protocol |
| ( F ) (18) _____ | R. Computer Aided Design |
| ( M ) (19) _____ | S. Business to Business |
| ( K ) (20) _____ | T. Chief Executive Officer |

## B Dictation

*Task One:* Listen to the short passage twice and fill in the blanks with the missing words or sentence.

### Answering phone calls

There are times when the phone calls (or the people on the line) can be too (1) _____. Being polite doesn't mean you have to (2) _____ your own time or drop whatever you are doing. If you are (3) _____ or answering someone else's phone, it is your responsibility to be as (4) _____ and helpful as possible, including (5) _____. (You shouldn't be answering someone else's phone if you aren't going to take the time to (6) _____.) However, if someone calls you at home or catches you in the middle of (7) _____, it is fine to offer to call him/her back. You can say, for example, "I'm sorry, but I was just about to run out of the door. (8) _____"

*Task Two:* You're going to hear five sentences. Repeat each sentence you hear. Then listen again and write down each sentence. Check your answer when you listen for the third time.

(1) _____

(2) _____
(3) _____
(4) _____
(5) _____

## ❻ Conversations

**Conversation 1**

*Task One:* Listen to the conversation and choose the best answer to each question.

(1) Who made the telephone call?
    A. Henry Wilson.                  B. Henry Andrews.
    C. Robert Andrews.              D. Robert Wilson.

(2) Where is Henry Wilson?
    A. In the office.                    B. At the table.
    C. In a department.              D. At a meeting.

(3) What is Robert's telephone number?
    A. 53802986.                     B. 53820986.
    C. 58302896.                     D. 53820968.

(4) When can Henry Wilson probably get the message?
    A. In about an hour.            B. Immediately.
    C. The day after tomorrow.    D. When he calls Robert.

(5) Who is the receiver of the phone call?
    A. She's Henry Wilson's customer.
    B. She's Henry Wilson's secretary.
    C. She's Robert Andrews' customer.
    D. She's Robert Andrews' secretary.

*Task Two:* Listen to the conversation again and decide whether the following statements are true (T) or false (F).

(1) Henry Wilson answers the phone call. (　　)
(2) The caller waits for half an hour to talk to Henry Wilson on the phone. (　　)
(3) Henry Wilson works in the marketing department. (　　)
(4) Robert Andrews will be on a meeting in an hour. (　　)
(5) The caller leaves a message for Henry Wilson. (　　)

**Conversation 2**

*Task One:* Listen to the conversation and check(√) the correct piece of information.

| The man | (1) Yes and mentioned | (2) Yes, but not mentioned | (3) No |
|---|---|---|---|
| has received a new catalogue. | ☐ | ☐ | ☐ |
| wants to get a sample of one of the products. | ☐ | ☐ | ☐ |
| is charged 100 dollars for the sample. | ☐ | ☐ | ☐ |
| gives the woman his address. | ☐ | ☐ | ☐ |
| will receive a sample sent by the woman. | ☐ | ☐ | ☐ |

*Task Two:* Listen to the conversation again and answer the following questions.

(1) Why does the man make the phone call?

(2) What item on the catalogue is the man interested in?

(3) How can the man get a free sample of the item he's interested in?

(4) Why does the man want to get a sample?

(5) Will the man have to pay the sample charge if he places an order of a hundred pieces?

## D Passage

*Task One:* Listen to the passage and decide whether the following statements are true (T) or false (F).

(1) Good phone manners are important only at work. (　)
(2) Answering the phone in a polite way is important to make a good impression. (　)
(3) Offering to take a message when answering the phone for someone else is good manners. (　)
(4) To let people know who they've reached as soon as they pick up the phone can make a person sound polite. (　)
(5) Always answering the phone in a particular way can make others feel comfortable. (　)

*Task Two:* Listen to the passage again and check (√) the correct piece of information.

| Good phone manners | (1) Yes and mentioned | (2) Yes, but not mentioned | (3) No |
|---|---|---|---|
| Saying the right things | ☐ | ☐ | ☐ |
| Speaking loudly | ☐ | ☐ | ☐ |
| Letting others know who they've reached immediately | ☐ | ☐ | ☐ |
| Some good phone manners can be learnt | ☐ | ☐ | ☐ |
| Answering the phone with "Who is this?" | ☐ | ☐ | ☐ |

# Part 4  Fun Listening

*Task:* Listen to the following tongue twisters and read them after the recording.

(1) Sixty-six sick chicks.
(2) The sixth sick sheik's sixth sheep's sick.
(3) She sells seashells by the seashore.
(4) Amidst the mists and coldest frosts, with barest wrists and stoutest boasts, he thrusts his fist against the posts, and insists he sees the ghosts.
(5) Betty Botter bought a bit of butter, "But," she said, "this butter is bitter, if I put it in my batter, it will make my batter bitter, but a bit of better butter will make my batter better." So Betty Botter bought a bit of better butter, and it makes her batter better.

# Unit 2 When would be good for you

## Unit Goals
◇ Making an appointment
◇ Changing an appointment
◇ Understanding time cultures
◇ Understanding airport announcements

## Part 1 Practical Listening & Speaking

### A Word study

Work with your partner to fill in the blanks using the words on the left. Listen and check your answers, and then follow the recording.

| make an appointment |
| convenient |
| check |
| diary |
| tied up |
| make it |
| suits |
| pick...up |
| agency agreement |
| delayed |

(1) I'm afraid I can't see you tomorrow. Could we _____ _____ _____ for our meeting?

(2) Could you ask someone to _____ me _____ at the airport?

(3) I think Tuesday _____ me best. See you on Tuesday.

(4) Would it be possible to _____ _____ our Tuesday meeting _____ Monday morning?

(5) I'd like to talk about the _____ _____ with you.

(6) The trip was _____ for one week because of the bad weather.

(7) I'm sorry. I'm _____ _____ all day on Friday.

(8) Let me _____ it on my computer. Sorry, I can't find it.

(9) I'm afraid I can't _____ _____ on Tuesday. I'm busy on that day.

(10) Could we _____ our meeting for the same time on Friday?

13

| |
|---|
| reschedule |
| heavy schedule |
| bring forward... to |
| fix another date |

(11) When would be _____ for you to visit us?

(12) Let me have a look at my _____. I think I'm free on that day.

(13) Today I have got a _____ _____. I will have to visit 6 clients.

(14) I would like to _____ _____ _____ with Mr. Hunter for tomorrow morning.

## B Functional listening

*Task One (Making an appointment)*: Listen to the recording and fill in the blanks.

May: Good morning. May Wang speaking.

Paul: Good morning, Ms. Wang. This is Paul Gray from KIP in London.

May: Hi, Mr. Gray. How are you?

Paul: Pretty good. And you?

May: I'm fine. Thanks.

Paul: I was wondering if (1) _____.
We have some new products which I think you might be interested in.

May: OK. When would be convenient for you?

Paul: How about June 5th?

May: (2) _____. Sorry, I'm afraid I'm tied up on that day.

Paul: Then could we make it the following day? That's Tuesday, June 6th.

May: June 6th (3) _____. What time would you like to come?

Paul: My flight will get into Shanghai at 9 a.m. Could we say 11 o'clock?

May: 11 o'clock would suit me very well. (4) _____ at the airport?

Paul: Thank you. That would be great.

May: Could you send us (5) _____
_____?

Paul: Sure. Then I'm looking forward to seeing you soon. Goodbye.

May: Goodbye.

*Task Two (Changing an appointment)*: Listen to the telephone conversation and complete the following notes using one or two words from the recording.

14  Unit 2  When would be good for you

(1) Paul is ringing about his appointment with May at 11 a.m. on _____ _____. He can't make it.
(2) Paul's _____ has been _____ for four hours, and he has a feeling that it may be longer than that.
(3) Paul wants to _____ the _____ for the same time on June 7$^{th}$.
(4) Paul is sorry for the _____ and thanks May for being so _____.

## C Language check

Work with your partner to complete the following expressions, and then listen and check your answers.

*Task One: Making an appointment*

*Introducing and asking to speak to someone*

F: Hello, this is Amy Wang calling from PPC. (1) _____ I speak to Alex Wells, please?
M: Alex Wells (2) _____.

*Making small talk*

F: Hi, Mr. Wells, how are you?
M: Fine, thanks. (3) _____ as usual.

*Asking to visit someone and mentioning the purpose*

F: I was wondering if I could (4) _____ you sometime in the near future. I'd like to give you a demonstration of our new product.
M: Sure. That would be (5) _____.

*Suggesting the visiting date*

F: So when would be (6) _____ for you? (When would be good for you?)
M: I will be in next week most of the time.
F: How about next Monday, April 4$^{th}$?
M: Let me check my (7) _____. Sorry, I'm afraid I'm tied up on that day.
F: Then could we make it the (8) _____ day? That's Tuesday, April 5$^{th}$.
M: April 5$^{th}$ suits me (9) _____. (April 5$^{th}$ would be best for me.)

*Suggesting the visiting time*

F: Then what time would you like me to come? (Then what time should I come?) Shall we (10) _____ 3 p.m.? (Could we say 3 p.m.?)
M: 3 p.m. is good for me. Let's make it then.

*Thanking and promising to confirm by email*

F: Thank you. That's very (11) _____ of you. I'll send you an email to confirm the visit right away.
M: OK. I'm looking forward to seeing you soon. Goodbye.

### Task Two: Changing an appointment

*Mentioning the change*

M: Hello, Jenny. I'm ringing (calling) about our appointment on July 6th at 10 a.m. I'm (1) _____ I can't make it. Something's come up.
F: Oh, that's a (2) _____. What happened?

*Mentioning the reason*

M: There has been a big problem in our head office. I have to attend an important (3) _____ there.
F: Oh, I see. (Oh, that's a problem.)

*Suggesting the new date*

M: Could we (4) _____ our meeting for the same time on July 10th? (Could we fix another date for the meeting? How about bringing forward our July 11th meeting to July 10th?)
F: Sorry. I'm afraid I've (5) _____ another appointment on the morning of July 10th.

*Suggesting the new time*

M: Then (6) _____ about the afternoon?
F: The afternoon would be great.
M: Shall we say 3 p.m.? (Could we say 3 p.m.?)
F: Yes, that's (7) _____ for me.

*Confirming and apologizing*

M: Then I'm looking forward to seeing you on July 10th. I'm really sorry for the change.
F: It's (8) _____ all right. These things happen.
M: Thank you for being so (9) _____. Goodbye.
F: Bye.

# Unit 2

## D Controlled practice

Work with your partner to make a dialogue based on the following flow chart. Listen to the recording of a model answer, and then follow it.

| YOU — Caller | YOUR PARTNER — Called Person |
|---|---|
| Introduce yourself. | Offer to help. |
| Ask for an appointment with Mr. Hall. | Ask what it's about. |
| Discuss an agency agreement. | Ask when is good. |
| Suggest next week. | Disagree — Mr. Hall is away. Suggest the beginning of next month. |
| Agree. | Disagree — Mr. Hall is busy. |
| Suggest Monday, May 3rd. | Suggest Tuesday. |
| Agree. Suggest 10 a.m. | Agree. |
| Say "thanks" and end the call. | End the call. |

## E Business culture

Work with your partner to answer the following questions. Then listen to the recording and fill in the blanks.

(1) Are you a punctual (守时的) person? What would you feel if you were late for an appointment?

(2) Do you make appointments in small segments (部分) of time? What about English people?

(3) Do you do two jobs at a time? What about English people?

### Understanding Time Cultures

**Linear Time (直线时间型):** In the linear time culture, people do (1) _____ _____ at a time. English and German people and those who are from northwest Europe (2) _____ and work by a linear clock. They make appointments in (3) _____ segments (15 – 30 minutes) and don't like being late. They don't like putting off to (4) _____ what they can do today. When you work with them, you should respect their (5) _____. When you have a meeting with them, you should be on time for the meeting, focus on it and keep your talk (6) _____.

**Flexible Time (变通时间型):** In the flexible time culture, people do (7) _____ _____ at the same time. Those from Mediterranean (地中海) countries and Latin America (拉丁美洲) have flexible time cultures. For them, schedules are (8) _____ _____ than human feelings. They sometimes don't go to (9) _____ in order to meet family members. When you work with them, you should leave more time for the (10) _____. For example, you may tell them, "I'll wait in your office from 11:00 to 11:30."

*Cyclical Time*(轮回时间型): Most Asians(亚洲人) and Africans(非洲人) have cyclical time cultures. They believe that people can't control (11) _____. Instead, the cycle of life controls people and they must live in harmony(和谐) with nature. They believe relationships are very important in any (12) _____. When you work with them, you should (13) _____ _____ building relationships. You should also be on time and be patient.

# Part 2  Business Speaking

## A Pair work

**Task One:** Work with your partner to complete Sandy's description of her appointments with the correct prepositions(介词) provided in the following table. In four of the spaces no preposition is necessary. Describe Sandy's week schedule to your partner.

| in (the factory) | in (Paris) | in (Japan) |
| --- | --- | --- |
| in (the morning) | at (the factory) | at (lunch) |
| at (ten o'clock.) | at (a meeting) | at (the head office) |
| at (home) | at (the airport) | on (Friday) |
| on (holiday) | on (a business trip) | at/on (weekends) |
| to (a meeting) | for (a course) | |

(1) ___/___ today I'm having lunch _____ Joe Collins.

(2) ___/___ tomorrow morning _____ ten I'm going _____ a sales meeting.

(3) I'm visiting ___/___ the factory _____ Wednesday _____ the morning. _____ the afternoon, I will meet Jack Taylor _____ the head office.

(4) ___/___ this Thursday, I will visit a client from Beijing.

(5) _____ 8 a.m. _____ Friday I'm flying _____ Paris _____ France _____ a training course.

(6) _____ weekends, I have to attend the training.

(7) Next week, I will be _____ holiday.

*Task Two:* Work in pairs to practice using expressions for "*Making Appointments*". One asks the following questions on the left, the other answers them. After this practice, change the roles.

A: Could I visit you sometime in the near future?   B: Sure. When shall we meet?
A: Could we meet on July 3$^{rd}$?   B:
A: Then when would suit you? Could we make it the following day? That's Tuesday, July 4$^{th}$.   B:
A: What time would be convenient for you?   B:
A: Could we say 4 o'clock?   B:
A: Shall we meet for dinner?   B:

## B Role play

*Task One:* Role-play a telephone conversation according to the following situations. You will be in your partner's city on business next week. Look at your schedule below and arrange a time to meet.

A: I'm coming to your city next week for a few days. Could we set up a meeting?
B: Of course. When are you available?

Your schedule

| Monday | |
|---|---|
| June 13$^{th}$ | Morning: 9:30 flight arrives, go to Plaza Hotel<br>Afternoon:<br>Evening: Dinner with Margaret Lee |
| **Tuesday** | |
| June 14$^{th}$ | Morning: 10:00 meeting with Ron Mendez<br>Afternoon: Trade show — presentation 2:00 p.m.<br>Evening: |
| **Wednesday** | |
| June 15$^{th}$ | Morning: Trade show — presentations<br>Afternoon:<br>Evening: |
| **Thursday** | |
| June 16$^{th}$ | Morning: 8:30 flight departs |

Your partner's schedule

| *Monday* | |
|---|---|
| June 13th | Morning: Flight leaves 8:40 a.m. for a meeting |
| | Afternoon: |
| | Evening: Returning 7:05 p.m. |
| *Tuesday* | |
| June 14th | Morning: 9:00 Sales meeting |
| | Afternoon: |
| | Evening: 8:00 Dinner, Jackie's Restaurant |
| *Wednesday* | |
| June 15th | Morning: 11:00 interview, Brian Jackson |
| | Afternoon: 1:00 lunch with Burt Wells |
| | Evening: |
| *Thursday* | |
| June 16th | Morning: Meeting with John Johnson |

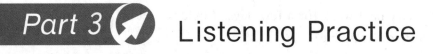

# Part 3  Listening Practice

## A Listening focus

**Airport announcements**

*Task One:* Listen to the announcement and choose the best answer to each of the questions.

(1) Who is probably making the announcement?
   A. A pilot.　　　　　　　　　　　B. A flight attendant.
   C. A ticket agent.　　　　　　　　D. A ground crew member.

(2) What is the ultimate destination of the flight?
   A. Atlanta.　　B. Miami.　　C. Caracas.　　D. Lima.

(3) What change has been announced?
   A. The flight number.　　　　　　B. The gate number.
   C. The arrival time.　　　　　　　D. The boarding time.

(4) What are the current weather conditions outside?
   A. It's raining.　　B. It's cloudy.　　C. It's freezing.　　D. It's windy.

(5) What time will the plane depart?
   A. 9:50 a.m.　　B. 12:15 p.m.　　C. 4:05 p.m.　　D. 8:45 p.m.

*Task Two:* Listen to the announcement and fill in the chart with what you hear.

| Departure time | |
|---|---|
| Flight No. | |
| Early boarding for | |
| Regular boarding | |

## B Dictation

*Task One:* Listen to the short passage twice and fill in the blanks with the missing words.

There is a theory of time that (1) _____ time into two distinct types.

One is monochronic time in which things are linear, and more importantly there is one thing (2) _____ at a time.

Another type is polychronic time in which a number of things can be happening at the same time, and (3) _____.

So in the sense of who is the (4) _____ and who is the master, in monochronic cultures like German and British culture, time is often the master. People are always (5) _____ time, and they have to manage time, and time seems to be always (6) _____ from people.

In polychronic cultures time is (7) _____. People are the masters of time, and so there's a much more (8) _____ approach and maybe more than one event occurring at the same time.

*Task Two:* You're going to hear five sentences. Repeat each sentence you hear. Then listen again and write down each sentence. Check your answer when you listen for the third time.

(1) _____
(2) _____
(3) _____
(4) _____
(5) _____

## C Conversations

**Conversation 1**

*Task One:* Listen to the conversation and match the people in Column A with the statements in Column B.

Column A                    Column B
Mr. Lee                     a) makes the phone call.
Mr. Jones                   b) answers the phone call.
                            c) is very busy on Wednesday morning.
                            d) is very busy on Friday.
                            e) has some trouble in using the spreadsheet.

Mr. Lee _____ , _____ , _____
Mr. Jones _____ , _____ , _____

*Task Two:* Listen to the conversation again and answer the following questions.

(1) Why has Mr. Lee been hoping to meet Mr. Jones?

(2) What problem does Mr. Lee have?

(3) How long will it take Mr. Jones to explain the formulas to Mr. Lee?

(4) When will Mr. Lee and Mr. Jones meet?

(5) When did Mr. Lee make this phone call?


**Conversation 2**

*Task One:* Listen to the conversation and decide whether the following statements are true (T) or false (F).

(1) John and Philip had decided to meet on Tuesday. (    )
(2) John now wants to cancel their meeting. (    )
(3) Philip hates to change an appointment and refuses to change it. (    )
(4) Thursday is convenient for John, but not for Philip. (    )
(5) Finally Philip is forced to postpone his meeting with John till Thursday. (    )

*Task Two:* Listen to the conversation again and match the people in Column A with the statements in Column B.

Column A                    Column B
Philip                      a) Thursday is convenient for him.
                            b) Tuesday is convenient for him.
John                        c) He wants to postpone the appointment.
                            d) He is sorry for changing the appointment.
                            e) He is considerate and can make it on Friday.

Philip: _____ , _____ ,
John: _____ , _____ , _____

22 ▎ Unit 2  When would be good for you

Unit 2

# D Passage

*Task One:* Listen to the passage and choose the best answer to each question.

(1) Why is one second in Beijing not the same as one second in Cairo?
    A. Because people have different attitudes to time.
    B. Because people experience time in different ways.
    C. Because people use different ways to measure time.
    D. Both A and B.
(2) Which of the following statements is true?
    A. Usually different attitudes to time may not lead to major problems.
    B. People can never understand how another culture works.
    C. 9 a.m. in Beijing actually means 1 p.m. in Cairo.
    D. Time has distressing effects on people.
(3) In which of the following situations do people need to adjust their attitude to time?
    A. When people come into a similar culture.
    B. When people come into a flexible culture.
    C. When people come into the U.K. or Germany.
    D. When a Briton (an Englishman) comes into a flexible culture.
(4) What is the main idea of this passage?
    A. Time is important since it is everywhere.
    B. The concept of time varies from culture to culture.
    C. People need to be punctual for meetings no matter what culture they are in.
    D. People from the U.K. or the U.S. always need to adjust their attitude to time.
(5) What's the speaker's tone?
    A. Subjective.    B. Negative.    C. Objective.    D. Ironic.

*Task Two:* Listen to the passage again and check (√) the correct piece of information.

|  | (1) Yes and mentioned | (2) Yes, but not mentioned | (3) No |
| --- | --- | --- | --- |
| Different attitudes to time always create major problems. | ☐ | ☐ | ☐ |
| If you want to be successful in cross-cultural communication, you should be aware of your attitude to time and sometimes you need to make some adjustment. | ☐ | ☐ | ☐ |
| In a flexible culture relationships are more important. | ☐ | ☐ | ☐ |
| A flexible culture is linear in time management. | ☐ | ☐ | ☐ |
| German culture focuses on getting things done in a short period of time. | ☐ | ☐ | ☐ |

CBE | 23

# Part 4　Fun Listening

*Task:* Listen to the song and sing along.

## Big Big World
### Emilia

I'm a big big girl
in a big big world
It's not a big big thing if you leave me
but I do do feel that
I too too will miss you much
miss you much...

I can see the first leaf falling
it's all yellow and nice
It's so very cold outside
like the way I'm feeling inside

I'm a big big girl
in a big big world
It's not a big big thing if you leave me
but I do do feel that
I too too will miss you much
miss you much...
Outside it's now raining
and tears are falling from my eyes
why did it have to happen
why did it all have to end

I'm a big big girl
in a big big world
It's not a big big thing if you leave me
but I do do feel that
I too too will miss you much
miss you much...

I have your arms around me ooooh like fire
but when I open my eyes
you're gone...

# Unit 3 Where would you like to stay

## Unit Goals
◇ Describing hotels
◇ Booking hotels for clients
◇ Understanding Chinese modesty culture
◇ Understanding directions and positions
◇ Making a reservation

## Part 1 Practical Listening & Speaking

### A Word study

Work with your partner to fill in the blanks using the words on the left. Listen and check your answers, and then follow the recording.

twin room

downtown area
a five-star hotel
Recreation facilities

squash court

fantastic gym
wireless Internet access
Catering

Room service
vacancy

(1) A _____ _____ is to or in the center or main business area of a town or city.
(2) A _____ _____ is a room that has two single beds.
(3) A _____ _____ has a bed for two people.
(4) _____ _____ is a service provided by a hotel, by which food and drinks can be sent to a guest's room.
(5) You can log on to the Internet here, because we have _____ _____ _____.
(6) I wish I could stay in _____ _____ _____.
(7) Excuse me, could you tell me where the check-in counter is? I'd like to _____ _____ _____ _____.
(8) _____ _____ are places or equipment for people to use to enjoy themselves.
(9) What's a _____ _____ like? Is there a meeting room?
(10) Squash is a game played by two people who use rackets to hit a small rubber ball against the walls of a _____ _____.

25

| |
|---|
| double room |
| daily rate |
| overlooks |
| balcony |
| business suite |
| check into a hotel |

(11) "What's the _____ _____?" "It's RMB 900 per night."

(12) It's a _____ _____. It has all kinds of equipment for doing physical exercise.

(13) Has your apartment got a _____?

(14) Let me see if we have a _____ for tonight. Sorry, we're booked up.

(15) _____ is the activity of providing food and drinks at parties, meetings, etc.

(16) If a house or room _____ something, it has a view of it, usually from above.

## B Functional listening

*Task One (Describing hotels):* Listen to the recording and fill in the blanks.

Sue: Sue Dai speaking. Can I help you?

Mike: Hi Sue, this is Mike Brown calling from PRK International in the U.K. I'm ringing about (1) _____ next week.

Sue: Oh, yes. How are you, Mr. Brown?

Mike: I'm fine, thanks. I wonder if you could book a hotel for me. I need a standard room (2) _____.

Sue: Yes, of course. Do you prefer any particular hotel?

Mike: I'd like to stay at a hotel in downtown area. Can you recommend one to me?

Sue: How about the Garden Hotel? (3) _____.

Mike: What's it like?

Sue: It's a five-star hotel. There are excellent recreation facilities. There is a bar, a swimming pool, tennis courts, squash courts, and a fantastic gym.

Mike: That sounds good. What (4) _____?

Sue: There is a business center in the hotel. They provide photocopying and typing services, wireless Internet access, and fax service. They also coordinate conferences and any catering which is included in them.

Mike: (5) _____?

Sue: Yes, I think so.

Mike: What about the distance to the airport?

Sue: It takes one hour to (6) _____.

Unit 3

Mike: That sounds great. Please book it for me.
Sue: OK. I will call them right away.
Mike: Thank you very much for your help.
Sue: It's a pleasure.
Mike: Well, I'm looking forward to seeing you soon. Goodbye.
Sue: Bye-bye.

**Task Two** (*Booking hotels for clients*): Listen to the recording and check (√) *True* or *False*.

|  | True | False |
|---|---|---|
| (1) The man wants to book a room from July 3 to 7. | ☐ | ☐ |
| (2) There are many rooms available in the hotel. | ☐ | ☐ |
| (3) There are three double rooms on the same floor. | ☐ | ☐ |
| (4) All the double rooms have a good view of the city. They have balconies and bathrooms. | ☐ | ☐ |
| (5) The man also wants to book a conference room for July 5. | ☐ | ☐ |

## ❸ Language check

Work with your partner to complete the following conversations. Then listen and check your answers.

### Task One: Describing hotels

*Recommending a hotel*

F: Would you mind booking a hotel for me? I need a (1) _____ room from 23 to 26 July.
M: Certainly. What kind of hotels would you like to stay at?
F: I'd like to stay at a hotel in (2) _____ area. Can you recommend one to me?
M: How about the Hilton Hotel?

*Asking about the hotel*

F: What's it (3) _____?
M: It's a five-star hotel. It's very pleasant.

*Asking about business facilities*

F: What are the (4) _____ facilities like there?

M: There is a business center. They provide such secretarial services as photocopying and typing. There is also wireless Internet (5) _____.

*Asking about recreation facilities*

F: What are the recreation facilities like there?
M: There are excellent recreation facilities — a spa, a swimming pool, a squash (6) _____ and a massage room.

*Asking about the distance to the airport*

F: How far is it to the airport?
M: It takes one hour to get to the International Airport by taxi.

*Asking about hotel services*

F: Do they provide (7) _____ _____?
M: Yes, I think so.

**Task Two: Booking hotels**

*Asking to book accommodation*

F: Good morning, Lucky Hotel. How may I help you?
M: Good morning, I'd like to book some (1) _____ for five nights.

*Asking for the room you want*

F: What kind of rooms would you like, sir?
M: I'd like to (2) _____ three double rooms for five nights, from May 1st to 5th.
F: Just a moment, let me (3) _____ my computer. Yes, we have three double rooms. They are all on the same floor.

*Asking about the daily rate*

M: What is the daily (4) _____?
F: Double rooms are RMB 500 per night.

*Asking about the room*

M: What are they like?
F: All the rooms are (5) _____ the city. They have a balcony and bathroom.
M: That would be fine.

*Giving the name and number*

F: Can I have your (6) _____ number, sir?
M: Yes, it's 46792345.
F: And your name, sir?
M: Steve Nash.

## Task Three: Checking into a hotel

*Offering help*

F: Good morning, sir. How may I help you?
M: Good morning, I have got a (1) _____. Can you check it, please?

*Asking for the guest's name*

F: Yes, of course. May I have your name, please?
M: My name is John Howard.
F: Just a second, please. Yes, we have your reservation. You are (2) _____ with us for 4 nights. Is that right?
M: Yes.

*Asking about the way of paying*

F: How would you like to pay (3) _____ your room, sir?
M: I'm going to pay by Visa. Here's my card.

*Asking the guest to complete the form*

F: Thanks. Now would you please (4) _____ in the form, sir?
M: OK.

*Offering help again*

F: May I help you with your (5) _____?
M: Yes, please. Thank you!
F: Your room is on the third floor. Here is your key. I hope you'll (6) _____ your stay with us.
M: Thank you.

## Task Four: Asking for hotel services

*Asking for room service*

F: Can I have room service?
M: Yes, of course. What kind of (1) _____ would you like, Continental or British style?
F: Continental style, please.
M: OK.

*Asking for a wake-up call*

F: I need a wake-up call tomorrow morning. Could you (2) _____ that for me?

M: Certainly. When would you like us to call you?
F: Please (3) _____ it 7 a.m.
M: OK. No problem.

*Asking for photocopying service*

F: Could you tell me where I can make some copies?
M: There's a (4) _____ room on this floor, just opposite the lobby.

*Asking for the long-distance call*

F: Can I make a long-distance call in the hotel?
M: Yes, of course. You can (5) _____ a long-distance call in your own room.

*Asking for laundry service*

F: Do you provide laundry service?
M: Yes. Do you need it (6) _____ now?
F: Not at the moment. Thanks.

## D  Controlled practice

You are a salesperson. Your partner is a client. Work together to make a telephone dialogue based on the following flow chart. Listen to the recording of a model answer, and then follow it.

| YOU | YOUR PARTNER |
| --- | --- |
| Introduce yourself and greet. | Introduce yourself and say you want to confirm the details about your trip. |
| Ask for his/her flight details. | Say arrival times in Shanghai. Ask him/her to meet you at the airport. |
| Agree. Offer to book a hotel for him/her. | Accept the offer. |
| Ask for his/her requirements of the hotel. | Say you need one close to the airport. |
| Ask if he/she needs a four-star or five-star hotel. | Say you need a four-star hotel. |
| Ask for his/her requirements about recreation facilities. | Say you don't have. |
| Ask for his/her requirements about business facilities. | Say you need one with a business center. |
| Ask for any other requirement. | Say "No, thanks." |

# E Business culture

Work with your partner to answer the following questions. Then listen to the recording and fill in the blanks.

(1) When Chinese people praise you, what's your usual response? What do you say to them?
(2) When Western people praise you, how will you respond? What should you say to them?
(3) What do you know about the Chinese modesty culture? Can you give an example?

---

**Understanding Chinese Modesty Culture**

Modesty(谦虚) is considered as one of the Chinese virtues(美德). When Chinese people talk about their achievements, the way of speaking should be modest. That means they should try to be humble(谦卑的) about their achievements, which is more (1) _____ in a Chinese social situation. If not so, they may be considered as boasting or proud and very likely to become the (2) _____ of gossip.

Compared with the Chinese, Westerners normally (3) _____ to take a factual approach when talking about what they have (4) _____. They will neither talk up nor talk down their achievements. They will just (5) _____ tell the truth. With this obvious cultural difference, they find it difficult to understand the Chinese modest way of speaking. Thus, very often (6) _____ occur. Here are two examples:

*Example One:* Once an American (7) _____ was invited to a Chinese party in a beautiful house. He was dazzled(使目眩) and even (8) _____ by the variety and sheer quantity of the food. On the table were (9) _____ of various kinds piled on top of already laid out ones. However, what was even more (10) _____ was the little speech given by the host: "Thank you very much for coming to my little humble house. We don't have good food for you, just several simple (11) _____ dishes and some common home-made (12) _____."

*Example Two:* Once an American who could speak a little Chinese was (13) _____ his Chinese friend's wedding. At the party, the American said to his friend in Chinese: "你的新娘很漂亮。(Your bride is very beautiful.)" To show his modesty, the Chinese said: "哪里！哪里！(Where? Where?)" The American was surprised and said: "每一个地方：鼻子、眼睛和皮肤。(Everywhere, the nose, the eyes and the skin.)"

# Part 2  Business Speaking

## A Pair work

*Task One:* Work in pairs to practice using expressions for "Describing Hotels". One asks the questions on the left, and the other provides an appropriate reply. After this practice, change roles. You may refer to "Language check".

A: What's the hotel like?  
B: It's a five-star hotel. It's very pleasant.

A: What are the business facilities like there?  
B:

A: What are the recreation facilities like there?  
B:

A: How far is it to the airport?  
B:

*Task Two:* Work in pairs to practice using expressions for "Booking Hotels". One says the sentences on the left, and the other provides an appropriate reply. After this practice, change the roles. You may refer to "Language check".

A: I'd like to book some accommodation for five nights.  
B:

A: I'd like four double rooms all on the same floor.  
B:

A: What is the daily rate?  
B:

A: What are the double rooms like?  
B:

A: Do you have a conference room I can book on May 7th?  
B:

## B Role play

*Task One:* Look at the pictures below. Take turns to describe the hotel-related things and people. Follow this dialogue.

A: What is a twin room?
B: A twin room has two single beds.

*Task Two:* You will stay in London on business for one week. Your partner has contacted the following three hotels there. Discuss together which hotel you will stay at.

A: Which hotel would you like to stay at?
B: I don't know. Can you describe them to me?

| | |
|---|---|
|  | ***Royal London Hotel*** (*five-star*)<br>　　Centrally located, the elegant Royal London is in Mayfair, near shops, parks, theatres and other attractions. The hotel has express check-in, 204 standard rooms and 42 work rooms with desks and communications facilities. The hotel also has a large lounge, health club and well-equipped fitness center.<br>**Standard double room 265 pounds per night** |
|  | ***St. Steven's Hotel*** (*three-star*)<br>　　In the heart of Theatreland, close to Covent Garden and only meters from Charing Cross, St. Steven's is comfortable and well-equipped, and it has an efficient and friendly service. There is a restaurant, a bar and free swimming pool access. The price includes a buffet breakfast.<br>**Price per person per night 56 pounds** |
|  | ***Hyde Park Gardens Hotel*** (*four-star*)<br>　　A quiet hotel, a short walk from Oxford Street and West End theatres, the Hyde Park Gardens has the famous Maritime Restaurant, an informal dining room and a full fitness center. It also offers a large buffet breakfast, afternoon tea in the lobby and a Sunday Jazz brunch.<br>**Price per person per night 97 pounds** |

# Part 3　Listening Practice

## A  Listening focus

**Directions & Positions**

*Task One:* Listen carefully and fill in the blanks with the missing words you hear on the tape.

(1) What does a compass show?
　　It shows _____.
　　What are the four points of the compass?
　　They are _____, _____, _____ and _____.

(2) What's east of the United States?
　　_____ is east of the United States.
　　What's west of the United States?
　　_____ is west of the United States.
　　New York is _____ of the United States.
(3) The shopping center is _____ of _____.
　　The school is _____ of _____.
　　The cinema stands _____ of _____.
　　The hotel stands _____ of _____.
　　The cinema stands _____ of _____.

*Task Two:* Listen to the statement and choose the correct picture to what you hear.

| | | |
|---|---|---|
| (1) Bill returned **to** his apartment. | A | |
| (2) Jack jumped **into** the pool. | B | |
| (3) David fell **onto** the floor. | C | |
| (4) The crab washed up **on** the shore. | D | |

| | |
|---|---|
| (5) Jean is **on** the floor. | E |
| (6) Michael is **in** the water. | F |
| (7) Drive **toward** the city limits and turn north. | G |
| (8) The plane headed **toward** a mountain. | H |
| (9) Take me **to** the airport, please. | I |
| (10) Dick jumped **on(to)** the mat. | J |
| (11) Athena climbed **onto** the back of the truck. | K |
| (12) The doctor is **in** his office. | L |

# B Dictation

*Task One:* Listen to the short passage twice and fill in the blanks with the missing words or sentence.

**Modesty**

We are (1) _____ think American culture and Chinese culture are much alike. In fact, their differences (2) _____ their similarities in our daily life. For example, in American and Chinese culture a hostess' responses to a (3) _____ are at polar opposites. An American hostess, complimented for her cooking skills, is likely to say, "Oh, (4) _____. I cooked it especially for you." But it's not so for a Chinese host or hostess (often the husband does the fancy cooking), who will instead apologize profusely for giving you "nothing" delicious to eat.

The most (5) _____ difference between American culture and Chinese culture is that the Chinese (6) _____ in "modesty"; the Americans in "straight forwardness". That (7) _____ has left many a Chinese hungry at an American table, for Chinese politeness calls for (8) _____ before one accepts an offer, and the American hosts take a "no" to mean "no", whether it's the first, second, or third time.

*Task Two:* You're going to hear five sentences. Repeat each sentence you hear. Then listen again and write down each sentence. Check your answer when you listen for the third time.

(1) _____
(2) _____
(3) _____
(4) _____
(5) _____

# C Conversations

**Conversation 1**

*Task One:* Listen to the conversation and decide whether the following statements are true (T) or false (F).

(1) The man wants to book a double room for his client and himself. (　)
(2) Unfortunately there's no single room available at the hotel. (　)
(3) The price of the room is 15 dollars per night. (　)
(4) There's a 10% discount of the room price. (　)
(5) The man doesn't book the room at the moment. (　)

*Task Two:* Listen to the conversation again and complete the table below.

## Room Reservation

| Requirement | A (1) _____ room with a (2) _____. (3) _____, away from the street. |
|---|---|
| Date | From (4) _____ to the morning of (5) _____. |
| Rate | (6) _____ per night. |
| Discount rate | (7) _____ for (8) _____. |
| Services | A radio, a (9) _____, a telephone and a major (10) _____. |

**Conversation 2**

*Task One:* Listen to the conversation and choose the best answer to each question.

(1) Why does the customer make the telephone call?
  A. Because he wants to book a holiday.
  B. Because he wants to take a brochure.
  C. Because he wants to get a discount.
  D. Because he is interested in the company.

(2) How does the customer get the information of this travel agency?
  A. He gets it from the newspaper.
  B. His friend tells him about it.
  C. He learns it from the brochure he took yesterday.
  D. He sees an advertisement on TV.

(3) What does the word "package" mean in this conversation?
  A. A parcel.                    B. A big box.
  C. Packing.                     D. A special kind of holiday.

(4) What is the total price of the holiday now?
  A. 858 dollars.                 B. 772.2 dollars.
  C. 154 dollars.                 D. 843 dollars.

(5) How much does the customer have to pay now if he wants to book the holiday?
  A. The total price.             B. 10 percent of the total price.
  C. 20 percent of the total price. D. 858 dollars.

*Task Two:* Listen to the conversation again and rearrange the following statements.

a) Filling in a booking form.
b) Enjoying the holiday.
c) Paying a deposit of 20%.

d) Getting a discount.
e) Paying the balance of 80% of the tour cost.

(1) _____ (2) _____ (3) _____ (4) _____ (5) _____

## D Passage

**Task One:** Listen to the passage and answer the following questions.

(1) Who reports to the speaker?

(2) According to the speaker, which department is the most important one in the hotel?

(3) Why is that department the most important one in the hotel?

(4) What is the most convenient way for people to book hotels?

(5) Why should the hotel provide information in simple English?

**Task Two:** Listen to the passage again and complete the table below.

| Name | (1) _____ |
|---|---|
| Post | (2) _____ of the Shang Ri-la Hotel in Shanghai |
| Responsibilities | a) Responsible for the (3) _____ of the hotel;<br>b) Setting managers of each department (4) _____;<br>c) (5) _____ certain standards are (6) _____;<br>d) Directly responsible for the (7) _____ department;<br>e) (8) _____ they are offering the right rates, at the right time and in simple English. |

# Part 4  Fun Listening

**Task:** Listen to the poem and try to translate it into Chinese.

## A Red, Red Rose
### Robert Burns

O My luve's like a red, red rose,
That's newly sprung in June;
O My luve's like the melodie,
That's sweetly play'd in tune.

As fair art thou, my bonnie lass,
So deep in luve am I;
And I will luve thee still, my dear.
Till a' the seas gang dry!

Till a' the seas gang dry, my dear,
And the rocks melt wi' the sun!
And I will luve thee still, my dear,
While the sands o'life shall run.

And fare thee weel, my only luve,
And fare thee weel a while!
And I will come again, my luve,
Though it were ten thousand miles!

# Unit 4 Welcome to our company

**Unit Goals**
◇ Meeting a client at the airport
◇ Receiving a client at the office
◇ Knowing eight questions you should not ask
◇ Identifying geographical locations
◇ Introducing a company

## Part 1  Practical Listening & Speaking

### A Word study

Work with your partner to fill in the blanks using the words on the left. Listen and check your answers, and then follow the recording.

| partnership |
| bumpy |
| representative |
| office |
| snack |
| downtown |
| baggage |
| business card |
| itinerary |
| worthwhile |
| After you |

(1) So shall we ____ ____ ____ ____?
(2) In our _____, you can find all kinds of products you like.
(3) Here is our _____ _____. You can have a break here at lunch hour.
(4) Wow, you've got a _____ office, but mine is very small.
(5) "This way, please." "_____ _____."
(6) We will try our best to make your visit interesting and _____.
(7) Your office building was very _____. It was big and special.
(8) Your _____ includes the bags and other things which you take with you when you travel.
(9) I'm not hungry now. I have just had a _____.
(10) Could you fax us your _____ once you have confirmed the trip?

41

| impressive |
|---|
| spacious |
| staff lounge |
| showroom |
| get down to business |

(11) Let me give you my _____ _____.

(12) I live _____, so it's very convenient for me to go shopping.

(13) We have a _____ _____ in Doha, Qatar. Please feel free to contact them if you need more information.

(14) The flight was not bad, but it was a bit _____.

(15) She worked in _____ with her sister. They shared the risks and profits.

## B Functional listening

*Task One (Meeting a client at the airport): Listen to the recording and fill in the blanks.*

Jane: Excuse me, are you Mr. Adams? My name is Jane Cheng. I'm from OPL Partnership.

Tom: Yes, I am. (1) _____.

Jane: It's my great pleasure to meet you too. Welcome to Shanghai.

Tom: Thank you. (2) _____.

Jane: My pleasure. Did you have a good flight?

Tom: It was OK. The flight was a bit bumpy but nothing was too bad.

Jane: Is this your first visit to Shanghai?

Tom: Yes. (3) _____, but never got to Shanghai. We have a representative office in Guangzhou.

Jane: Would you like something to drink or eat now?

Tom: No, thanks. I'm fine. (4) _____.

Jane: And is there anything else you'd like to do before we go downtown?

Tom: No, nothing else.

Jane: Can I help you with some of your baggage?

Tom: Oh, yes. Thank you.

Jane: Shall we go now? (5) _____.

Tom: OK. Let's go.

Jane: We'll go straight to your hotel — you're staying at the Hilton Hotel, I think. I will pick you up at around nine tomorrow morning. Amy Chen, our Sales Manager, will meet you at ten in our office.

Tom: (6) _____.

Task Two (*Receiving a client at the office*): Listen to the recording and check (√) *True* or *False*.

|  | True | False |
|---|---|---|
| (1) Mr. Adams has no business card. | ☐ | ☐ |
| (2) The offices in the building are very big. | ☐ | ☐ |
| (3) Mr. Adams would like to drink black coffee. | ☐ | ☐ |
| (4) Mr. Adams is only interested in the white models. | ☐ | ☐ |

## C Language check

Work with your partner to complete the following expressions, and then listen and check your answers.

### Task One: Meeting a client at the airport

*Greeting the client*

F: Excuse me, are you Mr. Bond? I'm Jenny Wang from the DDC Corporation.
M: Yes, I am. Pleased to meet you.
F: Pleased to meet you too. (1) _____ to Shanghai.
M: Thank you for coming here to collect me.

*Asking about the client's flight*

F: My pleasure. How was your (2) _____ ? (Did you have a good flight?)
M: Not too bad (Pretty tiring/ Exhausting)! Sorry I'm so late. There was a (3) _____ in New York. I hope you haven't been waiting too long.

*Asking about the client's visit*

F: It's OK. Is this your first (4) _____ to Shanghai?
M: No, this is my second trip to Shanghai.

*Offering a drink or snack*

F: Would you like to have a (5) _____ or something to eat before we go into town?
M: No, I'm OK.

*Asking anything else the client will do at the airport*

F: Then is there (6) _____ else you'd like to do before we set off?
M: No, thanks. Nothing else.

*Offering to help with the client's luggage*

F: Would you like me to help you with your (7) _____?
M: Yes, please. Thanks.

*Mentioning the client's hotel and schedule*

F: We'll go straight to your hotel. You're (8) _____ at the Garden Hotel, I think. I will pick you up at around nine tomorrow morning and then (9) _____ you to our factory.
M: Great.

**Task Two: Receiving a client at the office**

*Greeting and introducing*

F: Hi, Mr. Bond. It's my great pleasure to meet you. My name is Paula Chen. I work (1) _____ Amy Field.
M: It's very nice to meet you, too.

*Exchanging name cards*

F: Welcome to HDP. Let me give you my (2) _____ card.
M: And here is mine.
F: Thank you for (3) _____ the time to visit us. I know you have a busy itinerary.
M: It's a pleasure, Ms. Chen. I enjoy coming to your company.

*Offering drinks*

F: We'll do our best to make your visit (4) _____.
This is our meeting room. Please take a seat. Would you like something to drink? Tea or coffee?
M: Yes, thanks. Coffee would be nice. Black for me.

*Small talk: weather*

F: How do you (5) _____ the weather here?
M: It's pretty wet and cold.

*Showing the catalogue*

F: Yes, I agree. Would you like to have a look at our (6) _____ first or visit our showroom first?
M: The catalogue first.

## D Controlled practice

Work in pairs to make a dialogue. You say the sentences on the left, and your partner provides a proper reply. There is an example for you. After this practice, change roles. Then listen to the recording of a model answer, and follow it.

| YOU | YOUR PARTNER |
|---|---|
| Excuse me, are you Ms. Joan Brown? I'm James Li from HDP Partnership. | |
| It's very nice to meet you too, Ms. Brown. | Thank you for coming here to pick me up. |
| My pleasure. How was your flight? | |
| Is this your first visit to Guangzhou? | |
| Would you like something to drink or eat first? | |
| Is there anything else you'd like to do before we set off? | |
| Can I carry one of your bags? | |
| Shall we go now? My car is outside. | |

## E Business culture

Work with your partner to answer the following questions. Then listen to the recording, and fill in the blanks.

(1) Do you often ask your Chinese colleagues or friends the eight questions in the following article?
(2) Have you ever asked your Western colleagues or friends any of the eight questions? If you did, how did they answer you?
(3) Why should you not ask Westerners (西方人) these questions? Why do Chinese people often ask these questions?

### Knowing Eight Questions You Should Not Ask

When you are having a small talk（闲聊）with most Western business people, you should try not to ask them the following eight questions.

◇ **How old are you?** Age is a (1) _____ to most Westerners, especially those above 25. Obviously, this is a taboo（禁忌）(2) _____ for small talk.

◇ **How much do you make?** Salary（薪水）is another taboo topic in Western (3) _____. Even close friends don't know each other's salary and seldom talk about it.

◇ **How much does it cost?** Price is also a bad topic for small talk. If you ask your Western (4) _____ or (5) _____ this question, you may hear an answer like this: "I don't know. Someone gave it to me."

◇ **Are you married?** You should not ask about their marriage (6) _____ you are very close to them. Otherwise, they will probably say: "I'd rather not talk about my marriage."

◇ **Where do you live?** To most Westerners, home is a very private (7) _____, and they will not easily tell you where exactly they live unless they are (8) _____ to invite you to their home.

◇ **Are you Catholic（天主教徒）?** Most Westerners take their religion（宗教）(9) _____. If you don't know them very well, it's wise not to ask them this question.

◇ **Where are you going?** Chinese people often ask the question when (10) _____. To Westerners, they might think you are intrusive（侵犯的）, and you will probably get an answer: "I'm afraid it's (11) _____ of your business."

◇ **Have you had your dinner?** This question puzzles（困惑）many Westerners. They don't (12) _____ why their Chinese colleagues and friends often ask them this question. Unless they are told the (13) _____, they might think you would like to invite them to dinner.

# Part 2  Business Speaking

## A Pair work

*Task One:* Read the following conversation taking place at the airport. Work with your partner to put it into the correct order, and then practice it.

(1) Hello. Are you Rita Brown?

(2) It's good to meet you at last. I'm Ted Anderson from HDC. We spoke on the phone.

(3) Can I take one of your bags?

(4) It takes about an hour to get there. I have a car waiting outside. Is this your first time in Guangzhou?

(5) Oh really? How was the flight? It must have been very long for you.

(6) How long will you stay in Guangzhou?

A. It wasn't bad, but it was a bit bumpy.

B. Yes. Actually, it's my first time outside America.

C. About two weeks.

D. Yes, that was yesterday morning. Nice to meet you, too.

E. Yes, that's right. Hello.

F. Oh, yes please. Thank you. Is it far to your office?

*Task Two:* Work with your partner to put the sentences below into pairs. Then decide which pairs of sentences would be used by people meeting for the first time. Which would be used by people who have met before? Which could be used by both? Complete the table.

(1) Hello. I'm Sarah Nicholson.

(2) It was nice to meet you.

(3) How is your job going?

(4) How are you doing?

(5) Would you like a coffee?

(6) Hello, nice to see you again.

A. Hello, good to see you too.

B. Yes, please. That would be nice.

C. Pretty good. And you?

D. It's going well. How about yours?

E. Hi. I'm Edward Lee.

F. Nice meeting you too.

| First time | Met before | First time and met before |
|---|---|---|
| (1) — ___<br>(2) — ___ | (4) — ___<br>(6) — ___ | (3) — ___<br>(5) — ___ |

## B Role play

***Task One:*** You are a host and your partner is a visitor. You are meeting for the first time. Make a conversation according to the following prompts(提示).

| ◇ Introduce yourself.<br>◇ Shake hands.<br>◇ Give your business card.<br>◇ Offer a seat.<br>◇ Offer a drink.<br>◇ Ask about her hotel, trip, the length of her stay in Shanghai. | ◇ Introduce yourself.<br>◇ Shake hands.<br>◇ Accept the card and give your business card.<br>◇ Accept the seat.<br>◇ Accept a drink.<br>◇ Answer the questions and ask about the local weather. |
|---|---|

***Task Two:*** You are a host and your partner is a visitor. You have met before and know each other well. Make a conversation according to the following prompts.

| ◇ Greet your visitor. Ask how she is.<br>◇ Shake hands.<br>◇ Offer a seat.<br>◇ Offer a drink.<br>◇ Ask about her job and her stay in Shanghai. | ◇ Greet your host and answer his question.<br>◇ Shake hands.<br>◇ Accept the seat.<br>◇ Accept a drink.<br>◇ Answer the questions. |
|---|---|

***Task Three:*** Use some of the words in the table below to complete Jack's description of his experiences of taking a plane. You may change the form of some verbs. Then imagine you were Jack and describe your experiences to your partner.

(1) After getting my ticket in the _____ _____, I went to get my boarding pass.
(2) Then, I checked in my _____.
(3) Next, I checked in and went through the security _____.
(4) Following that, I went through the _____.
(5) Then, I waited 40 minutes in the airport _____, which was close to my boarding gate.
(6) I _____ the plane at 8:30 p.m. I was lucky to have a window seat, and the air hostesses were really beautiful.
(7) The plane _____ at Shanghai International Airport at 10:00 p.m. It was a long flight, and I was jet lagged.
(8) Finally I went to _____ my baggage.

| boarding pass<br>登机卡 | duty-free shop<br>免税店 | boarding gate<br>登机口 | air hostess<br>空姐 |
| --- | --- | --- | --- |
| security check<br>安检 | claim one's baggage<br>认领行李 | cabin<br>客舱 | airport lounge<br>候机室 |
| carry-on luggage<br>手提行李 | jet lagged<br>因时差产生的劳累 | check-in counter<br>验票台 | check in one's baggage<br>托运行李 |
| customs<br>海关 | conveyor belt<br>传送带 | steward<br>男乘务员 | stewardess<br>女乘务员 |
| board a plane<br>登机 | economy/business class<br>经济(商务)舱 | land<br>着陆 | life jacket<br>救生衣 |
| seat belt<br>安全带 | flight number<br>航班号码 | booking office<br>售票处 | return (round-trip) ticket<br>往返票 |

# Part 3  Listening Practice

## A Listening focus

**Geographical locations**

*Task One:* Listen to the recording and mark out on the map the three places: a) Prince Street; b) Royal Road; c) the post office. Draw a route to the post office from the train station.

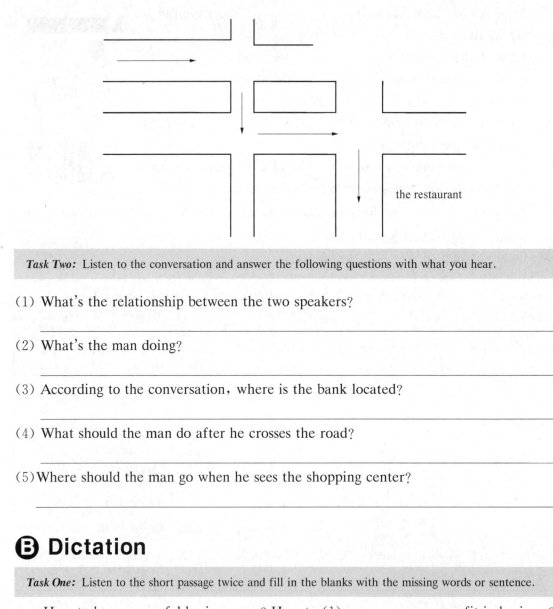

**Task Two:** Listen to the conversation and answer the following questions with what you hear.

(1) What's the relationship between the two speakers?

(2) What's the man doing?

(3) According to the conversation, where is the bank located?

(4) What should the man do after he crosses the road?

(5) Where should the man go when he sees the shopping center?

## B Dictation

**Task One:** Listen to the short passage twice and fill in the blanks with the missing words or sentence.

How to be a successful businessman? How to (1) _____ more profit in business? These are the issues that (2) _____ every businessman. A successful businessman not only needs to be (3) _____ the business world but also needs to learn something about the culture his partner belongs to. Asking personal affairs is a (4) _____ between Chinese and English cultures. People from China do not regard others' age, (5) _____, wages, personal life, belief and (6) _____ as personal affairs. While westerners will think you (7) _____ their right of privacy. Therefore, when we talk to the westerners, we must avoid asking the following eight questions:

"How old are you?"

"Are you married?"

"How many children do you have?"

"How much do you earn?"
"What's your weight?"
"Do you go to church?"
"Do you support the Democratic Party?"
"(8) _____?"

*Task Two:* You're going to hear five sentences. Repeat each sentence you hear. Then listen again and write down each sentence. Check your answer when you listen for the third time.

(1) _____
(2) _____
(3) _____
(4) _____
(5) _____

## C Conversations

**Conversation 1**

*Task One:* Listen to the conversation and choose the best answer to each question.

(1) What does Peter think of his flight?
   A. It was terrible.　　　　　　　　B. It was comfortable.
   C. It was fast.　　　　　　　　　　D. It was tolerable.

(2) Which of the following statements is true?
   A. It is Peter's first visit here.
   B. Peter doesn't like the place.
   C. Peter came to the city last year.
   D. Peter could clearly remember the name of the hotel where he stayed last year.

(3) What does Peter think of the place he stayed at last year?
   A. He enjoyed his stay.　　　　　　B. He thought it was tolerable.
   C. It didn't mean much to him.　　 D. He didn't like it at all.

(4) Is the accommodation important, according to Peter?
   A. Yes, it can make traveling tolerable.
   B. Yes, he always wants the best accommodation.
   C. No, it doesn't mean much to him.
   D. No, he can stand any kind of accommodation.

(5) Where does the conversation probably take place?
   A. At the headquarters.　　　　　　B. At the airport.
   C. At the railway station.　　　　　D. In the office.

**Task Two:** Listen to the conversation again and match the people in Column A with the statements in Column B.

Column A
Peter Chen
Matthew Jones

Column B
a) travels on business.
b) comes to meet a client.
c) came to the city last year.
d) has reserved a room at the Peace Hotel.
e) couldn't remember the name of the hotel.

Peter Chen _____ , _____ , _____
Matthew Jones _____ , _____ , _____

**Conversation 2**

*Task One:* Listen to the conversation and check (√) the correct piece of information.

| David Johnson... | (1) Yes and mentioned | (2) Yes, but not mentioned | (3) No |
|---|---|---|---|
| has made an appointment with Mr. Zhang | ☐ | ☐ | ☐ |
| is from an import and export company | ☐ | ☐ | ☐ |
| is extremely busy at the moment | ☐ | ☐ | ☐ |
| has found a problem in the contract | ☐ | ☐ | ☐ |
| is eager to talk about the contract with Mr. Zhang | ☐ | ☐ | ☐ |

*Task Two:* Listen to the conversation again and rearrange the following statements.

a) He finds a problem in the contract.
b) He is asked to examine the contract.
c) He is ushered to the office.
d) He comes to the company to discuss the problem.
e) He takes a seat and waits for a moment.

(1) _____ (2) _____ (3) _____ (4) _____ (5) _____

## D Passage

*Task One:* Listen to the passage and rearrange the following statements.

a) We only employed 20 employees at the beginning.
b) I'd like to introduce some of our key products to you.
c) We're building a new factory.
d) We hope to do business together.
e) We produce and sell products in more than thirty countries.

(1) _____ (2) _____ (3) _____ (4) _____ (5) _____

*Task Two:* Listen to the passage again and complete the table below.

| | Introduction of the Company |
|---|---|
| History | It was founded in (1) _____ with a (2) _____ of only 50 thousand U.S. dollars.<br>There were only 20 employees, half of whom were (3) _____. |
| Present Situation | There are 500 employees.<br>We (4) _____ products in more than 30 countries on (5) _____.<br>We produce and sell (6) _____ products each year, and the annual (7) _____ rate is at least 6 percent for the next five years.<br>A new factory is being built in one of the (8) _____ in China. |
| Products | There is (9) _____ products.<br>We supply (10) _____ and cables to meet all the needs. |

# Part 4   Fun Listening

*Task:* Listen to some advice about life and appreciate it.

## Words to Live by
（生活的忠告）

I'll give you some advice about life.

Do more than others expect you to do and do it pains;

Remember what life tells you;

Don't take to heart every thing you hear. Don't spend all that you have. Don't sleep as long as you want;

Whenever you say "I love you", please say it honestly;

Whenever you say "I'm sorry", please look into the other person's eyes;

Find a way to settle, not to dispute;

Never judge people by their appearance;

Speak slowly, but think quickly;

When someone asks you a question you don't want to answer, smile and say, "Why do you want to know?"

Call your mother on the phone. If you can't, you may think of her in your heart;

If you fail, don't forget to learn your lesson;

Remember the three "respects". Respect yourself, respect others, stand on dignity and pay attention to your behavior;

Whenever you make a phone call smile when you pick up the phone, because someone can feel it!

Find time for yourself;

Life will change what you are but not who you are;

Remember that silence is golden;

Read more books and watch less television;

The harmonizing atmosphere of a family is valuable;

When you quarrel with a close friend, talk about the main dish, don't quibble over the appetizers;

Figure out the meaning of someone's words;

Treat our earth in a friendly way, don't fool around with Mother Nature;

Go to a place you've never been to every year;

Remember, not all the best harvest is luck;

Do the thing you should do.

# Unit 5 What would you like for the starter

## Unit Goals
◇ Dining in a Western restaurant
◇ Making, accepting and declining invitations
◇ Understanding Western table manners
◇ Understanding lines, angles and shapes

## Part 1　Practical Listening & Speaking

### A Word study

Work with your partner to fill in the blanks using the words on the left. Listen and check your answers, and then follow the recording.

| |
|---|
| gin and tonic |
| white wine |
| soda water |
| starter/appetizer |
| main course |
| avocado |
| prawn |
| steak |
| rare |

(1) What would you like for the _____?

(2) _____ is the same as shrimp. The former is British English; the latter is American English.

(3) "How would you like your _____ done?" "Medium well, please."

(4) If meat is _____, it has only been cooked for a short time and is still red.

(5) _____ is a small sea creature that you can eat. It has a flat round shell made of two parts that fit together.

(6) "Would you like some coffee?" "Yes, that would _____ _____ _____."

(7) _____ is an alcoholic drink made from a mixture of different drinks. It is also a mixture of small pieces of fruit.

(8) _____ is a list showing what you have eaten and how much you must pay. It's called "bill" in British English.

(9) _____ _____ _____ is an alcoholic drink made with gin and tonic served with ice and a thin piece of lemon.

| |
|---|
| scallop |
| cocktail |
| dessert |
| hit the spot |
| check |
| beverages |

(10) _____ are hot and cold drinks.
(11) What would you like for the _____ _____?
(12) _____ is a fruit with a thick green or dark purple skin that is green inside and has a large seed in the middle.
(13) _____ is sweet food served after the main part of a meal.
(14) Would you like _____ _____ or red wine?
(15) Can I have it with _____ _____?

## B Functional listening

*Task One* (*Dining in a Western restaurant*): Listen to the recording and fill in the blanks.

Waiter: Good evening. Would you like something to drink first?
Linda: That's a good idea. Sam, (1) _____?
Sam: I'll have a gin and tonic.
Waiter: OK.
Linda: I'll (2) _____ and soda.
Waiter: So one gin and tonic and one white wine and soda.
Linda: Yes, thank you.

(*In a few minutes*)

Waiter: (3) _____, Madam?
Linda: Yes. Sam, what would you like for the starter and main course?
Sam: I'd like to have the avocado and prawns for starters. And I think I'll (4) _____ _____.
Waiter: How would you like your steak, sir? Well done, medium well, medium, medium rare, or rare?
Sam: Oh, medium, please.
Linda: Hmmm, I don't think (5) _____.
I'll just have the main course. Let me see. I think I'll give the scallops a try.
Waiter: Yes, madam. So, one avocado and prawn cocktail, one medium steak, and scallops.
Linda: That's right.

(*In a few minutes*)

Sam: Well, (6) _____.
Linda: I'm glad you enjoyed the food. Would you like some dessert?
Sam: No, thanks. I couldn't eat another bite.
Linda: Well, how about coffee?
Sam: Oh, yes, please. (7) _____.

(*In a few minutes*)

Linda: Excuse me, the check, please.
Waiter: Here it is, thank you.
Sam: Can I get this?
Linda: No, no, certainly not, this one's mine.
Sam: OK. Thanks. I'll pay next time when you come to Florida.

*Task Two* (*Making, accepting and declining invitations*): Listen to the conversation and complete the following notes using one or two words from the recording.

(1) The man says next Tuesday evening does not _____ him.
(2) The man says he can _____ it next Friday evening.
(3) The woman says it will take _____ _____ to walk to her home.
(4) The woman suggests the man take a _____.
(5) The woman will _____ the man her address.
(6) The woman says there will be a German _____ at the dinner.

## ⓒ Language check

Work with your partner to complete the following conversations. Then listen and check your answers.

### *Task One: Dining in a Western restaurant*

*Beverages*

F: Would you like something to drink first?
M: That's a good idea. I'll have a (1) _____ wine.

*The menu*

F: Shall we have a look at the (2) _____?
M: OK.

*Starters* (*U.K.*)/*appetizers* (*U.S.*)

F: What would you like (3) _____ the starter?
M: I'd like to have the shrimp cocktail for the starter.

*Salads*

F: What (4) _____ of salad would you like?
M: I'll have the spinach salad.

*Main courses* (U.K.) /*entrées* (U.S.)

F: (5) _____ would you like for the main course?
M: I'll try the steak for the main course.
F: How would you (6) _____ your steak?
M: Medium well.

*Side dishes*

F: What side dish would you like (7) _____ that?
M: Hmm. I think I'll have mixed vegetables.

*Desserts*

F: Would you (8) _____ for some dessert?
M: No, thanks. I'm full.

*Tea or coffee*

F: (9) _____ about coffee?
M: Oh, yes, please. That would hit the spot.

*The bill* (U.K.) /*check* (U.S.)

M: Let me pay (10) _____ this.
F: No, no, certainly not. I will get this. This one is mine.
M: OK. Thanks. Then I'll pay next time when you come to New York.
F: Great. I'm looking forward to that.

**Task Two: Making, accepting and declining invitations**

*Inviting someone to dinner/party*

◇ Would you like to have dinner in my home sometime next week?
◇ I'd like to invite you to dinner in my home sometime next week.

*Finding out when*

◇ That (1) _____ great. When exactly?
◇ That's very kind of you. When exactly?

*Suggesting a date/time*

◇ Would next Tuesday evening (2) _____ you?
◇ How about next Wednesday evening?

*Saying you're busy*

◇ I'm afraid I can't (3) _____ it next Wednesday evening.
◇ Unfortunately I'll be on a business trip on that day.

*Suggesting another date/time*

◇ That's a pity. Is next Friday evening (4) _____ for you?
◇ How about next Friday at 7 p.m.?

*Agreeing with the time and finding out **where***

◇ That's (5) _____ for me. Where do you live? Is it far?
◇ Friday 7 p.m. would be great. How can I get there?

*Suggesting a taxi*

◇ It's not really far. It'll take about 30 minutes on (6) _____.
◇ Well, I'd suggest that you take a taxi. It's a lot easier.

*Finding out **who***

◇ How many (7) _____ will be there?
◇ Can you tell me who will be at the party?

## D Controlled practice

You are a host. Your partner is a visitor to your company. Work together to make a dialogue based on the following points. Listen to the recording of a model answer, and then follow it.

| YOU | YOUR PARTNER |
|---|---|
| Ask your visitor if he/she has tried the local cuisine. | Say no—but you've heard it is very good. |
| Agree—describe a particular specialty. | Comment. |
| Suggest a meal in a restaurant. | Accept. |
| Respond. Ask if he/she likes fish. | Say yes—you have heard that the fish in this town is very good. |
| Confirm this view. Suggest you'll meet him/her at the hotel. | Respond. Ask what time. |
| Suggest a time. | Agree. |
| Confirm the arrangement and end the conversation. | End the conversation. |

## E Business culture

Work with your partner to answer the following questions. Then listen to the recording and fill in the blanks.

(1) Have you ever had a Western dinner before? If you did, what did you eat?
(2) Do you know any Western table manners? What are they?
(3) Do you know any differences between the Chinese and Western dinner? What are they?

**Understanding Western Table Manners**

*Using a napkin:* At the beginning of a dinner, unfold the napkin and put it on your lap, as this gesture will be (1) _____ anywhere. If you're at an extremely formal dinner and your napkin (2) _____ to the floor, signal a staff member so that he can pick it up and bring a fresh one. Finally, when leaving the table after the meal, the napkin should be (3) _____ placed beside the plate.

*Holding utensils（餐具）:* According to the European (4) _____, the fork will remain in the left hand and the knife in the right. But in America, people often set the (5) _____ down on the plate and transfer the (6) _____ to the right hand. Whether you use the American Style or European Style, it's important to never cut more than one or two (7) _____ at a time.

*Use of utensils:* Start with the knife, fork, or spoon (8) _____ from your plate, work your way in, using one utensil for each (9) _____. If the soup is served, remember to spoon away from yourself. This helps stop the drips. Do not put the (10) _____ soup spoon in your mouth. Instead, fill a soup spoon about 75 per cent with soup, and sip（吸吮）it from the side (11) _____.

*Eat with your fingers:* Bread must always be (12) _____ and never cut with a knife; other foods you can eat with your fingers include cookies, French fries, fried chicken, and hamburgers, (13) _____ and small fruits.

*Inedible（不可食用的） food:* When eating meat with a fork, you have to use that fork to (14) _____ the unwanted fatty piece. An exception to this rule is fish. It is fine to remove tiny bones with your (15) _____, because it would be difficult to drop them on a fork.

*Other tips:* Chew with your mouth (16) _____ and don't make noise. Don't talk with your mouth full. Don't pick something out of your teeth. If possible, try not to burp or (17) _____ at the table. Do not put your elbows on the table. Do not put bones or anything else on the table. Things that are not eaten should be put on your plate.

# Part 2  Business Speaking

## A Pair work

**Task One:** Read the conversation below. Work with your partner to put it into the correct order, and then practice it.

Unit 5

(1) Welcome to our restaurant. Do you have a reservation?

A. Dry white wine, please.

(2) Will this table do for you?

B. I think I will try the steak.

(3) Here is the menu. Are you ready to order?

C. Well done, please.

(4) Yes, of course. These are the starters, these are the main courses and these are the desserts.

D. Chocolate cake, please.

(5) The Chef's salad is a specialty of this region.

E. What's the specialty in this restaurant? What do you recommend?

(6) What would you like for the starter?

F. Yes, that's fine.

(7) What would you like for the main course?

G. No, I'm afraid I don't.

(8) How would you like your steak done?

H. OK. Can you help me with the menu?

(9) Would you like some dessert?

I. I'll have the fish soup.

(10) What would you like to drink?

J. OK, I'll try that.

*Task Two:* Your partner is going to attend a Western dinner party and ask for your advice on it. Read the advice in the table below and choose some for your partner.

A: What should I pay attention to when attending a Western dinner party?
B: I think you should bring a small present to the host or hostess.

| | | |
|---|---|---|
| (1) Bringing a small present to the host or hostess | (2) Eating with your mouth closed | (3) No spitting food on the table |
| (4) No persuading people to eat (helping yourself to food) | (5) No persuading people to drink wine or liquor | (6) Ordering or choosing your own food |
| (7) No talking too loud | (8) Being not wasteful | (9) Splitting the bill if there's no host |

## B Role play

***Task One:*** Your partner is a visitor to your hometown. You have invited him/her to a restaurant. Use the menu and wine list below. Ask what your partner would like to eat.

A: What would you like for the starter?
B: I think I'll have the prawn cocktail.

| MENU | | SIDE DISHES | |
|---|---|---|---|
| **STARTERS** | | Baked potato | £ 3.50 |
| Prawn/shrimp cocktail | £ 3.00 | Mashed potatoes | £ 4.50 |
| Chef's soup of the day | £ 3.50 | French fries | £ 3.50 |
| French onion soup | £ 3.00 | Noodles | £ 2.50 |
| Fruit cup/fruit cocktail | £ 2.50 | Mixed vegetables | £ 5.50 |
| Potato skins | £ 2.50 | **DESSERTS** | |
| Fish soup | £ 3.50 | Chocolate cake | £ 2.50 |
| **MAIN COURSES** | | Apple pie | £ 4.00 |
| **FISH** | | Pudding | £ 2.50 |
| Rainbow trout, grilled with almonds | £ 10.50 | Ice cream sundae | £ 4.50 |
| Poached cod with creamy mushroom sauce | £ 9.50 | Hot apple pie with cinnamon and raisins | £ 3.50 |
| Grilled Gulf shrimp | £ 14.50 | **WINE LIST** | |
| Broiled fish | £ 16.50 | **Before your meal** | |
| **MEAT** | | Sherry | £ 3.00 |
| Roast lamb | £ 15.50 | Gin, whiskey, vodka, rum | £ 4.50 |
| Baked chicken | £ 9.50 | Aperitifs | £ 3.50 |
| Sirloin steak topped with mustard seeds | £ 16.50 | Cocktails | £ 3.50 |
| Traditional roast beef with Yorkshire pudding | £ 19.50 | Beer, lager, draught | £ 5.00 |
| Grilled lamb chops stuffed with chicken livers | £ 13.50 | Soft drinks, fruit juices | £ 1.50 |
| Veal cutlets with rosemary and apple | £ 10.00 | **With your meal** | |
| **SALADS** | | **WHITE WINE** | Half bottle |
| Seafood platter (prawn, lobster, crab, white fish) | £ 8.50 | Chablis (dry, crisp, long-flavored) | £ 10.50 |
| | | Riesling (medium-dry, light, fragrant) | £ 14.00 |
| Honey-baked ham with pineapple relish | £ 9.50 | **RED WINE** | Half bottle |
| Tomato salad with garlic and herbs | £ 5.50 | Bordeaux AOC (rich, powerful, full-bodied) | £ 12.50 |
| Mixed Basque salad | £ 7.50 | **After your meal** | |
| | | Liqueurs | £ 4.90 |
| Greek salad | £ 4.50 | Tea, coffee | £ 6.50 |

**Task Two:** Western food is somehow different from Chinese food. Make a list of Western food that you would like to eat. Practice describing it to your partner. Use the expressions in *Table One* and the words in *Table Two*.

*Table One*

| It's a local specialty. | It's very popular here. | It's a kind of vegetable/fruit. |
| It's a bit like… | It's fairly hot/quite rich. | It's very sweet. |
| It's salty. | It's from Italy. | The main ingredients are… |

*Table Two*

| *Dairy products* (乳制品) | | |
|---|---|---|
| low-fat milk(低脂牛奶) | skim milk(脱脂乳) | chocolate milk |
| cheese(奶酪) | butter(黄油) | margarine(人造黄油) |
| sour cream(酸奶油) | yog(h)urt(酸奶) | |
| *Packaged foods* (包装食品) | | |
| macaroni(通心面) | cereal(谷类食品) | cookie(甜饼干) |
| cracker(饼干) | spaghetti(意式细面条) | noodle(面条) |
| *Juice and beverages* (果汁和饮料) | | |
| apple juice(苹果汁) | pineapple juice(菠萝汁) | grapefruit juice(柚子汁) |
| tomato juice(番茄汁) | grape juice(葡萄汁) | fruit punch(果汁宾治) |
| lemonade(柠檬汁饮料) | orange juice(橘子汁) | soda(苏打水) |
| *Poultry* (家禽) | | |
| chicken(鸡肉) | thigh(鸡腿) | drumstick(家禽的腿下部) |
| chicken breast(鸡胸) | chicken wing(鸡翅) | turkey(火鸡) |
| salami(意大利腊肠) | ham(火腿) | pork(猪肉) |
| duck(鸭肉) | beef(牛肉) | |

续 表

| Meat | | |
|---|---|---|
| bacon(咸肉，熏肉) | roast(大块烤肉) | steak(牛排) |
| stewed meat(炖肉) | leg of lamb(羊腿) | lamb chop(羊排) |
| pork chop(猪排) | rib(猪肋排) | sausage(香肠) |
| *Seafood*(海鲜) | | |
| salmon(三文鱼) | trout(鲑鱼) | crab(蟹) |
| swordfish(旗鱼) | whitefish(鲑鱼) | shrimp(虾) |
| *Seafood and shellfish*(海鲜和甲壳类动物) | | |
| oyster(牡蛎) | scallop(扇贝) | lobster(龙虾) |
| mussel(贻贝) | clam(蛤) | crayfish(小龙虾) |
| *Snack foods*(小吃) | | |
| potato chip(薯片) | popcorn(爆米花) | nut(坚果) |
| corn chip(玉米片) | peanut(花生) | nacho chip(烤干酪辣味玉米片) |
| *Condiments*(调料) | | |
| ketchup(番茄酱) | mustard(芥末) | relish(香料，佐料) |
| pickle(盐汁，醋汁，泡菜) | olive oil(橄榄油) | spice(香料，调味品) |
| mayonnaise(蛋黄酱) | vinegar(醋) | salad dressing(色拉调料) |
| *Coffee and tea* (饮料) | | |
| decaffeinated coffee(除去咖啡因的咖啡) | cappuccino(热牛奶卡布契诺咖啡) | herbal tea(花草茶) |

# Part 3 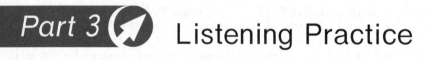 Listening Practice

## A  Listening focus

**Understanding Lines，Angles & Shapes**

*Task One:* Match the following words of shapes with the pictures and write the words in the blanks according to the definitions you hear.

Unit 5

| rectangle | cube | triangle | diamond | oval | cylinder |
| heart | square | crescent | circle | star | sphere |

| 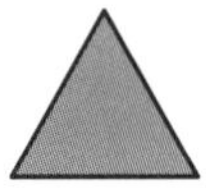 A _____ | B _____ | 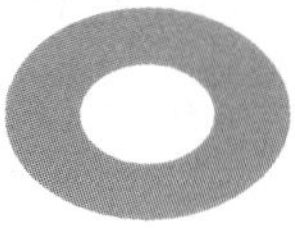 C _____ |  D _____ |
|---|---|---|---|
| 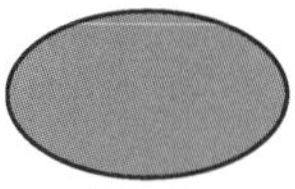 E _____ |  F _____ |  G _____ |  H _____ |
|  I _____ | 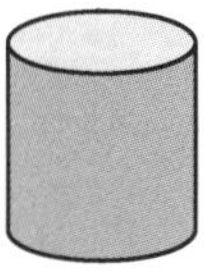 J _____ | 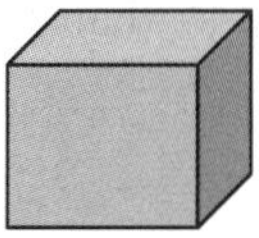 K _____ | L _____ |

**Task Two:** Listen to the explanations of the lines or angles and complete the following with what you hear.

| | |
|---|---|
| (1) You can only draw one line between two points. You will not be able to draw a second line through points *A* and *B*. |  |
| (2) There's 360° around a _____. Draw a circle please. | |
| (3) Two lines can intersect at ONLY one point. *S* is the only intersection of $\overline{AB}$ and $\overline{CD}$ in the figure below. Put down *S* please. | 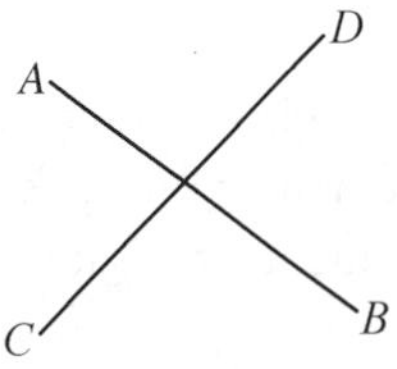 |

| | |
|---|---|
| (4) A line segment has ONLY one midpoint. $M$ is the only Midpoint of $\overline{AB}$ in the figure below. Put down $M$ in the proper place. | 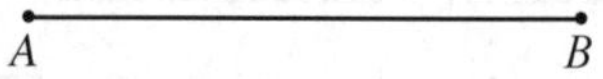 $A \rule{3cm}{0.4pt} B$ |
| (5) A line segment will always be the shortest distance between two points on a plane. The curved line and the broken line segments are further in distance between $A$ and $B$. Draw the line of the shortest distance between $A$ and $B$. |  |
| (6) An _____ measures less than 90°. Draw an acute angle. | 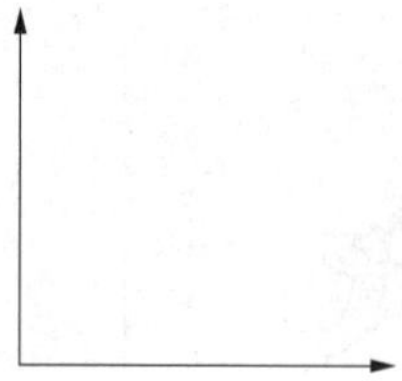 |
| (7) A right angle measures exactly 90°. Draw a right angle. | |
| (8) An obtuse angle measures more than 90° but less than 180°. Draw an obtuse angle. | |
| (9) A reflex angle is more than 180° but less than 360°. Draw a reflex angle. | |
| (10) Two angles adding up to 180° are called supplementary angles. Please point out the supplementary angles in the following. | 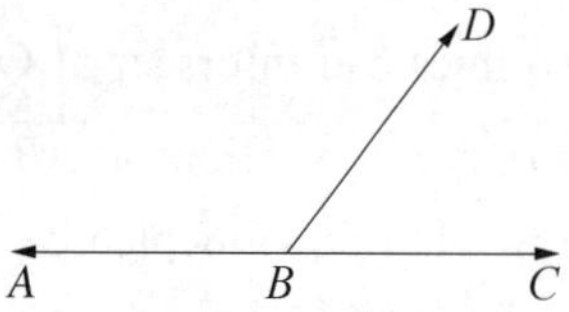 |

66 ▎ Unit 5  What would you like for the starter

# Unit 5

## B Dictation

*Task One:* Listen to the short passage twice and fill in the blanks with the missing words or sentence.

Do you ever eat out? I think the answer is "Yes". There are some (1) _____ between western (2) _____ and ours. If you don't know the do's and don'ts of (3) _____, you will be (4) _____. Let's learn more about Western (5) _____. Then, you will enjoy eating out.

- Don't pick up the soup bowl and drink from it.
- Don't (6) _____ the table for some kind of food. Please ask someone to pass a dish to you.
- Don't put bones on the table. Just leave them on your plate.
- (7) _____.
- Don't use your napkin to (8) _____ your face. Just put it on your lap.

*Task Two:* You're going to hear five sentences. Repeat each sentence you hear. Then listen again and write down each sentence. Check your answer when you listen for the third time.

(1) _____
(2) _____
(3) _____
(4) _____
(5) _____

## C Conversations

**Conversation 1**

*Task One:* Listen to the conversation and choose the best answer to each question.

(1) Where does this conversation most likely take place?
 A. At a park. B. At a restaurant.
 C. At a birthday party. D. At a music recital.
(2) Which section do they prefer?
 A. Smoking section. B. Non-smoking section.
 C. Whatever comes open first. D. Either one.
(3) How many people are talking in the conversation?
 A. One. B. Two. C. Three. D. Four.
(4) How long do they have to wait according to the waiter?
 A. 5 Minutes. B. 9 Minutes. C. 8 Minutes. D. 10 Minutes.
(5) Which is NOT true according to the dialogue?
 A. At first there is no vacancy in the non-smoking section.

B. Before the customers get the seats they are asked to wait for a while.
C. The waiter is very polite.
D. The customers begin to order immediately.

*Task Two:* Listen to the conversation again and write down five questions asked by the waiter.

(1) _____
(2) _____
(3) _____
(4) _____
(5) _____

## Conversation 2

*Task One:* Listen to the conversation and choose the best answer to each question.

(1) What does the woman invite William to do?
   A. Watch TV.              B. Have a drink.
   C. Have dinner.           D. Go skating.
(2) What does the man invite William to do?
   A. Watch TV.              B. Have a drink.
   C. Have dinner.           D. Go skating.
(3) What does William originally plan to do tomorrow night?
   A. Watch TV.              B. Have a drink.
   C. Have dinner.           D. Go skating.
(4) When will William go skating?
   A. Tonight.               B. Tomorrow night.
   C. The day after tomorrow. D. Someday next week.
(5) What is the most probable relationship between these three people?
   A. Teacher and students.  B. Classmates.
   C. Brothers and sister.   D. Supervisor and subordinators.

*Task Two:* Listen to the conversation again and dictate the beginning part.

Hillary: _____
William: _____
Hillary: _____
William: _____
Hillary: _____

## D Passage

*Task One:* Listen to the passage and decide whether the following statements are true (T) or false (F).

(1) The etiquette of dining can show a person's character. (    )
(2) If you are the host of a meal, you should ask your guests what they want to have and follow their ideas. (    )
(3) Once your guests arrive, you should appear as if you have waited for a long time to show your politeness. (    )
(4) The guest should never be late. (    )
(5) The host should settle the bill without the guest's presence. (    )

*Task Two:* Listen to the passage again and complete the table below.

| The Etiquette of Dining ||
|---|---|
| The host | The guest |
| (1) In scheduling the meal, just pick two restaurants, pick two different hours, and _____. <br> (2) A day before the meal, check with your guest to _____ the date, time and _____. <br> (3) Greet your guest _____ with a _____ when he or she arrives. | (1) Arrive at least five, but no more than 10 minutes _____ your _____. <br> (2) Keep your voice _____ and _____. <br> (3) Don't overload the _____ with your personal accessories. |

# Part 4　Fun Listening

*Task:* Listen to the song "Skater Boy" and sing along.

### Skater Boy
**by Avril Lavigne**

He was a boy
She was a girl
Can I make it any more obvious

He was a punk
She did ballet
What more can I say

He wanted her
She'd never tell secretly she wanted him as well
But all of her friends
Stuck up their nose
They had a problem with his baggy clothes
He was a skater boy
She said see you later boy
He wasn't good enough for her
She had a pretty face
But her head was up in space
She needed to come back down to earth
5 years from now
She sits at home
Feeding the baby she's all alone
She turns on TV
Guess who she sees
Skater boy rockin' up MTV
She calls up her friends
They already know
And they've all got
Tickets to see his show
She tags along
Stands in the crowd
Looks up at the man that she turned down
He was a skater boy
She said see you later boy
He wasn't good enough for her
Now he's a super star
Slamming on his guitar
Did your pretty face see what he's worth?
Sorry girl but you missed out
Well tough luck that boy's mine now
We are more than just good friends
This is how the story ends
Too bad that you couldn't see,
See the man that boy could be
There is more that meets the eye
I see the soul that is inside
He's just a boy
And I'm just a girl
Can I make it any more obvious
We are in love
Haven't you heard
How we rock each other's world
I'm with the skater boy
I said see you later boy
I'll be back stage after the show
I'll be at the studio
Singing the song we wrote
About a girl you used to know

# Unit 6 This is our new showroom

## Unit Goals
◇ Describing a product in the showroom
◇ Explaining the catalogue
◇ Understanding personal space
◇ Understanding public signs

## Part 1 Practical Listening & Speaking

### A Word study

Work with your partner to fill in the blanks using the words on the left. Listen and check your answers, and then follow the recording.

selling points
design
fine craftsmanship
customized services
quotation
complaints
durable
shipping time
units
brochure stands

(1) These are the _____ _____. They are $ 300 each.
(2) These are the _____ _____. They are $ 500 each.
(3) Why do you think your products are better? What are their _____ _____?
(4) I have several _____ about the hotel room. First, it's very noisy. I could not sleep at all last night.
(5) This pair of shoes is very _____. You can wear them for a long time.
(6) I'm afraid your _____ is a bit high. Could you give us the lowest one?
(7) This chair is of the latest _____. It's very popular with customers.
(8) Could I _____ this model _____ you? It's the latest.
(9) Do you provide _____ _____? I'm afraid what we need is a bit different from what you have here.
(10) We can produce 600 _____ per month.

| |
|---|
| budget ones |
| luxury ones |
| recommend...to |

(11) Our products are famous for their _____ _____. Please take a look at this one. It's very carefully made.

(12) What about _____ _____? When can you deliver the goods to us?

(13) Please have a look at these _____ _____. They are very well made.

## B Functional listening

*Task One (Describing a product in the showroom)*: Listen to the recording and fill in the blanks.

Peg: This way please. This chair is the latest model.
Sam: (1) _____. So what are the selling points of this model?
Peg: It's designed in the German style. (2) _____. It has got fine craftsmanship, and the quality of the material is excellent.
Sam: (3) _____. What's it made of?
Peg: It's made of real wood.
Sam: And where is it produced?
Peg: It's produced in (4) _____.
Sam: Can you provide customized services?
Peg: Yes, certainly. We can produce all kinds of chairs according to customers' requirements.
Sam: How long is your warranty period?
Peg: Our warranty period is 5 years. By the way, I'd like to tell you that (5) _____ from our customers. Our products are very durable.
Sam: What about the delivery time?
Peg: It depends on the size of your order. If you order 200 units of this model, we can finish producing them within two weeks. Including the one-month shipping time, (6) _____ the goods to your company.
Sam: OK. Could I have a look at other products?
Peg: Sure. Could you come this way, please?

*Task Two (Explaining the catalogue)*: Listen to the recording and check (√) *True* or *False*.

Unit 6

|  | True | False |
|---|---|---|
| (1) The buyer is not interested in chairs. | ☐ | ☐ |
| (2) The buyer would like 20 budget brochure stands and 30 luxury brochure stands. | ☐ | ☐ |
| (3) The buyer would like 10 units of BS123 Workstation. | ☐ | ☐ |
| (4) The seller will send their lowest quotation to the buyer by 6 January. | ☐ | ☐ |

## C Language check

Work with your partner to complete the following conversations, and then listen and check your answers.

### Task One: Describing products

*Talking about the selling points*

M: What are the selling (1) _____ of this model?
F: It has got fine craftsmanship, and it has a reasonable price and excellent quality. It's great (2) _____ for money.

*Talking about raw materials*

M: What's it made of?
F: It's (3) _____ of imported metal. It's very strong.

*Talking about measurements*

M: What are its measurements (尺寸)?
F: The measurements are 204 cm (4) _____ 100 cm.
M: What about the height?
F: The height is 250 cm.

*Talking about the production place*

M: (5) _____ is it produced?
F: It's produced in our Guangzhou factory.

*Talking about the customized service*

M: Can you provide customized service?
F: Yes, we can produce all kinds of (6) _____ according to customers' requirements.

*Talking about the delivery time*

M: What about delivery time?
F: If you (7) _____ 200 units, we can finish producing them within 3 weeks. Including the one-month shipping time, it will take 50 days to (8) _____ the goods to your company.

CBE | 73

*Task Two: Explaining the catalogue*

*Asking the customer's preference*

M: Thank you for showing me around the showroom.
F: You're welcome. Shall we have a look at the (1) _____ ? Which products are you interested in?
M: Could you (2) _____ to page 3? I'm interested in these three chair models. I'd like 50 units for each model.
F: Let me write down the (3) _____ numbers. What about the brochure stands on page 5? How many would you like?
M: OK. I would like twenty (4) _____ ones and thirty luxury ones.

*Recommending products*

F: Could I recommend BX123 to you? Its style is (5) _____ for your office. (Would you like to have BX345? It's very popular with customers.)
M: OK, I'd like to have 10 units of BX123.

*Promising to send a quotation*

F: Is there anything else you'd like?
M: No, that's all for the (6) _____. When could you give us a quotation (7) _____ these products?
F: We can send you a quotation by January 4th.

*Task Three: Comparing products*

◇ BX123 is much cheaper than BX234.
◇ It's (1) _____ convenient to use than that one.
◇ It's lighter than that one.
◇ It has a (2) _____ warranty than that one.
◇ It has a (3) _____ delivery time than that one.
◇ This thing is a lot (4) _____ to use than a video camera.
◇ This one has the lowest price.

## D Controlled practice

You are the seller, and your partner is the buyer. Make a dialogue based on the following prompts (提示). Listen to the recording of a model answer, and then follow it.

Unit 6

| YOU |
|---|
| Selling points of this model? |
| Production material? |
| Length(长度)? |
| Width(宽度)? |
| Height(高度)? |
| Customized service? |
| The place of production? |
| Warranty period? |
| Delivery time? |

| YOUR PARTNER |
|---|
| Excellent craftsmanship. Durable. |
| Real wood. |
| 150 cm. |
| 80 cm. |
| 100 cm. |
| Yes. |
| Our Shanghai factory. |
| 3 years. |
| 30 days. |

## E Business culture

Work with your partner to answer the following questions. Then listen to the recording, and fill in the blanks.

(1) Do you ever feel angry with someone who stands too close to you?
(2) Do you feel comfortable when someone on the bus shouts into his mobile phone or the colleague sitting next to you uses some strong perfume(香水) you don't like?
(3) How do you understand personal space?

### Understanding Personal Space

Where we sit, or how close we stand to other people when we talk, can be very (1) _____ _____ one culture to another. This is because people have different personal space.

Americans generally prefer more personal space than people in Mediterranean and Latin American cultures. American (2) _____ _____ usually prefer about (3) _____ feet between speakers when talking. However, comfortable (4) "_____ _____" for Latin Americans is about one and a half feet away from the other person.

The distance between speakers also depends on their (5) _____. Edward Hall, an expert in America, described the different distances between people when they are talking. He (6) _____ four kinds of distances (7) _____ people of different relationships: A. close friends (15 cm to 45 cm); B. good friends (45 cm to 120 cm); C. acquaintances(熟人) (1.2 m to 3.5 m); D. public distance (over 3.5 m). He said that different (8) _____ have different distances of personal space.

If you stand too (9) _____ to or too (10) _____ away from someone, you might give the wrong (11) _____. For example, some people might stand back to make (12) _____ _____. They are only moving into their comfortable personal space, but the other person might think this is (13) _____. What can you do? If you don't know about someone's customs, (14) _____ your own. But watch how the other person (15) _____. It probably won't be very long before you can get an idea about that person's comfortable personal space.

# Part 2　Business Speaking

## A  Pair work

*Task One:* Work with your partner to match the expressions in Part A with those in Part B. Use the matched expressions to describe your products to your partner.

|  | Part A | Part B |  |
|---|---|---|---|
| IKEA has | (1) the most competitive（有竞争力的） | A) warranty period (money-back guarantee). |  |
|  | (2) the lowest | B) customized service (quality). |  |
|  | (3) the longest | C) delivery time. |  |
|  | (4) the latest | D) service. |  |
|  | (5) the shortest | E) model/design. |  |
|  | (6) the best | F) range of products. |  |
|  | (7) the fastest | G) price. |  |
|  | (8) the widest | H) quotation. |  |

*Task Two:* Here are some useful expressions from this unit. Put the words in correct order. Then Student A asks the questions on the left, and Student B answers the questions. After the practice, change roles.

(1) points/ are/ What/ the/ this/ selling/ of/ model?　A.

(2) of/ What's/ made/ it?　B.

(3) its/ What/ measurements/ are?　C.

(4) produced/ is/ Where/ it?　D.

(5) customized/ provide/ Can/ you/ service?　E.

(6) about/ What/ time/ delivery?　F.

(7) the/ you/ recommend/ Could/ best/ one/ to/ us?　G.

(8) When/ give/ could/ you/ us/ a/ for/ products/ quotation/ these?　H.

Unit 6

## B Role play

You work for a company in Singapore. You want to send an important document to a very important customer in Thailand. The document must arrive before noon the next day. Which of the following three services should you use? Discuss with your partner.

A: Which service should we use?
B: I think NTN is the best because it's cheaper (the cheapest).

| | |
|---|---|
| **NTN Express**<br>◇ Road Express: 1-/2-3- or 4-day service<br>◇ To any country in S.E. Asia<br>◇ We guarantee the cheapest price!<br>◇ Call now: 986 5534. |  |
| **Delivery Force**<br>◇ A4 size from $50<br>◇ 10 pick-up points in Singapore<br>◇ Guaranteed next-day delivery (within office hours 9 a.m. - 6 p.m.)<br>◇ Most deliveries before noon in major cities<br>◇ Tel: 345 5633 |  |
| **Royal Star**<br>◇ Collecting and delivering documents to the door<br>◇ Guaranteed next-day delivery before 10 a.m.<br>◇ 3-day economy service also available<br>◇ Prices start at $90.<br>◇ Tel: 433 4522 |  |

# Part 3  Listening Practice

## A Listening focus
**Public Signs**

*Task One:* Look at the road signs below. Listen and match each sign with what you hear. Write in the brackets the letter and the name of the sign.

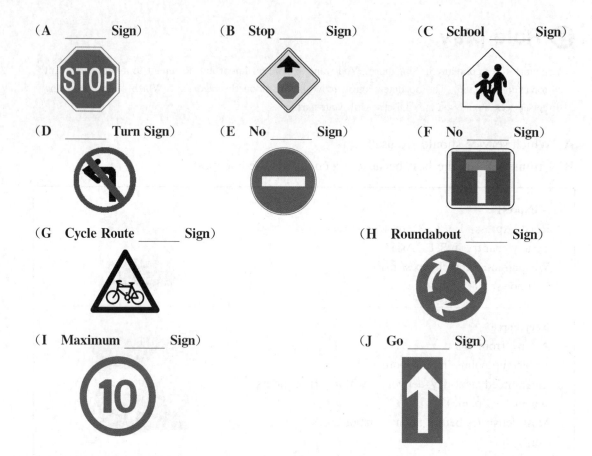

*Task Two:* Look at the following miscellaneous signs. Listen and match each sign with what you hear. Write in the brackets the letter of the sign and the name of the sign.

(1) Information sign is usually seen at airports, train stations and other public places where you can ask for information. (          )
(2) This is a no smoking sign. Cigarette smoking is not permitted where this sign is posted. (          )
(3) Warning Sign warns you of a dangerous road ahead. (          )
(4) No swimming signs are put where occasional undercurrents are active.
(          )
(5) This is a wet floor sign. You can see it in front of a building on rainy days.
(          )
(6) This is a Recreational and Cultural Interest Sign. It tells you there is a cinema, museum or an entertainment center around. (          )
(7) No littering sign reminds you not to litter anything around. (          )
(8) Construction Signs will tell you something is under construction which may bring you inconvenience. (          )
(9) This is a restroom sign. A restroom is a room with a toilet in it, especially in a public building. (          )
(10) Pets on Leash Sign tells that pets should be kept on a rope when they are out.
(          )
(11) A wet paint sign usually reminds you to be careful of the wet paint. (          )
(12) This illuminated sign will be hung above a doorway indicating a fire exit. They are often seen in hotels, cinemas, offices and other public places. (          )

## B Dictation

*Task One:* Listen to the short passage twice and fill in the blanks with the missing words or sentences.

### Product

Product is, of course, the thing (or service) that you have to offer to the (1) _____. There are a number of things about the product you should evaluate.
  (2) I _____.

### Product Description

It is critical to be able to say in one clear sentence why your product is perfect for a (3) _____ and what it does best.
  "To (4) _____, product name is the type of product that performs this task."

### Functionality, Features & Benefits

In order to begin to understand the product from a customer's point of view, list the functionality, the features, and (5) _____ that product has.
  List functionality and features that could (6) _____.

Prioritize each for the target market or market segments to (7) _____ the development of the product going forward.

(8) _____.

*Task Two:* You're going to hear five sentences. Repeat each sentence you hear. Then listen again and write down each sentence. Check your answer when you listen for the third time.

(1) _____

(2) _____

(3) _____

(4) _____

(5) _____

## C Conversations

**Conversation 1**

*Task One:* Listen to the conversation and choose the best answer to each question.

(1) What is the right position of the cars in the showroom?

◆Lancia; ●Mini; ■Citroen; ★Volvo

A. B. C. D.

(2) Which car is the most expensive one according to the conversation?
    A. The Mini.            B. The Citroen.
    C. The Peugeot.         D. The Toyota.

(3) Which feature of the cars is NOT mentioned in the conversation?
    A. Energy saving.       B. Nationality.
    C. Price.               D. Color.

(4) The woman does not choose the Mini because it _____.
    A. is expensive         B. is too small
    C. costs too much oil   D. doesn't have a radio

(5) The woman is probably interested in _____.
    A. the black Toyota     B. the red Toyota
    C. the Lancia           D. the Peugeot

*Task Two:* Listen to the conversation again and write the words you hear in the blanks.

M: Good afternoon, Madam. What can I do for you?

F: I'm interested in buying a car.
M: Do you have (1)_____?
F: Not really. But I think it should be energy saving.
M: How about the Mini (2)_____ between the Lancia and the Volvo? It costs ＄2,830 and is cheap (3)_____: it does 38 miles per gallon. Or there's the Citroen, behind the Mini. It is even cheaper to run: it does 45 miles per gallon and costs only ＄2,070. It's not (4)_____ though, it only does 69 miles per hour.
F: (5)_____ the Mini and the Citroen are too small. I've got (6)_____. Isn't there anything bigger?
M: Well, there's the Toyota over there, to the left of Peugeot. It's (7)_____ and cheap to run too, costing ＄3,040. It does only 36 miles per gallon and it also has a (8)_____ radio.
F: Well, I'll (9)_____. And what color are you offering? I don't like blazing red.
M: Oh, yes. We also have intense black and rainforest green for (10)_____.
F: Um, I think I'd like to see the black one.

**Conversation 2**

*Task One:* Listen to the conversation and fill in the chart with the missing information.

| Product name | _____ |
|---|---|
| Two varieties introduced | _____ and _____ |
| Material used | _____, with _____ in it |
| Burning hours | _____ or _____ hours |
| Minimum order | _____ pieces |
| Length of ship date | _____ days |

*Task Two:* Listen to the passage again and match the questions with the responses. F is the salesperson, while M is the customer.

M: Can I have a look at your catalogue?    (1) That's impressive.
F: _____
M: Um, burning approximately 25 hours...    (2) What's the minimum order?
F: _____
M: _____

F: 1,000 pieces, and it's the same with all the other models.
M: Well, the ice-cream candles look like real ice-creams.
F: _____
M: They light 80 hours, even longer than aromatherapy candles.
F: _____

(3) Yes, long enough for several romantic occasions, right?
(4) Sure. This is it.

(5) Right, they are a kind of gel candles.

## D Passage

*Task One:* Listen to the passage and mark the statements with:

Y (for YES) if the statement agrees with the information given in the passage;
N (for NO) if the statement contradicts the information given in the passage;
NG (for NOT GIVEN) if the information is not given in the passage.

(   ) (1) When two people are talking to each other, they try to be as close to each other as possible.
(   ) (2) Everybody has an invisible boundary, which may not be crossed by others.
(   ) (3) People back away when others are too close to them because closeness reduces intimacy.
(   ) (4) Men and women have different understanding of acceptable boundary.
(   ) (5) Never put your arm around anybody's shoulder, not even your closest friends.

*Task Two:* Listen to the passage again and complete the answers to the questions.

(1) Why do people tend to stand a specific distance apart when talking?
   Because there's a(n) _____ around their body.
(2) What would people do if others are too close to them when talking?
   They will move away to increase _____.
(3) What is special about personal space in American culture?
   Americans tend to require _____ than in other cultures.
(4) What suggestion does the speaker give when you find people to whom you are speaking back away?
   _____ close the gap.
(5) What problem would physical contact cause for casual acquaintances?
   It may lead to _____.

Unit 6

# Part 4  Fun Listening

**Task One:** Listen to the poem, and choose the situation that is NOT mentioned in it.

### When making a mistake

When applying for leave
When out of the office
When on a day off sickness

**Task Two:** Listen to the poem again and then put the explanation of each behavior into the two boxes marked *you* and *your boss* respectively.

A. must be very ill           B. going for an interview
C. always sick               D. on business
E. overworked                F. wandering around

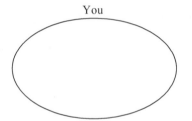

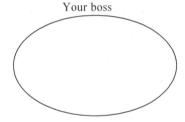

# Unit 7  Let me tell you more about our product

## Unit Goals

◇ Making a sales presentation
◇ Demonstrating a product
◇ Learning three *Ps* for presentations
◇ Making a sales presentation
◇ Understanding tips for a successful presentation

## Part 1  Practical Listening & Speaking

### A  Word study

Work with your partner to fill in the blanks using the words on the left. Listen and check your answers, and then follow the recording.

agents and distributors

world top 500

certificate
cost-effective
after-sales service

good value for money
functions and features
slides
cushion

(1) Our _____ _____ is excellent. We provide on-site maintenance service within 24 hours after receiving customers' call.
(2) The salesperson gave us a _____ of the machine to show how it worked.
(3) Don't _____ your chair back so far. It might fall over.
(4) If you buy a _____ product, you will save some money.
(5) You will enjoy other _____ if you buy this product. For example, we will give you a bag as a gift.
(6) So what are the _____ _____ _____ of this product? Could you show me how it works?
(7) Please have a look at the _____ of this chair. It's very soft. Please sit down and have a try.
(8) ADC is a multinational among the _____ _____ _____.
(9) We have obtained a _____ for this product from ISO. Here it is.

84

| tilt |
| benefits |
| demonstration |
| trustworthy |

(10) He is _____. You can trust him for any job.
(11) This machine is _____ _____ _____ _____.
You can't find any other product like this one.
(12) This chair _____ easily because its wheels are very smooth.
(13) We have many _____ _____ _____. They sell our products to customers from all over the world.

## B Functional listening

*Task One (Making a sales presentation):* Listen to the recording and fill in the blanks.

Good morning, and welcome to B & D Corporation. I'm Frank Hopson, the Sales Manager. (1) _____ some basic information about our company and products.

Now let me start with the company. B & D Corporation was founded in 1970. At that time, there were only 6 people working in the company, but now we (2) _____ in 12 countries. We also have many agents and distributors across the world. Our turnover increased from 5 million dollars in 1970 to 900 million dollars last year. More than half of our clients are (3) _____. They include BAYER, BMW, NOKIA, etc.

(4) _____. Now I'd like to tell you about our products. We have been specializing in office furniture for more than 35 years. We sell workstations, desks and all kinds of chairs, which are very cost-effective. All of them have got ISO's certificates. We also provide (5) _____. We promise to provide on-site maintenance within 24 hours after receiving our clients' call.

In conclusion, we are a trustworthy company. If you choose our products, you will find they are good value for money, and you will enjoy wonderful services from us. (6) _____, I will be happy to answer them now.

*Task Two* (*Demonstrating a product*): Listen to the recording and check (√) *True* or *False*.

|  | True | False |
|---|---|---|
| (1) The best thing about the chair is that it's cost-effective. | ☐ | ☐ |
| (2) The chair is not heavy and easy to carry. | ☐ | ☐ |
| (3) The chair is not suitable for training rooms. | ☐ | ☐ |
| (4) The chair has six colors. | ☐ | ☐ |

## ❸ Language check

Work with your partner to complete the following expressions, and then listen and check your answers.

*Task One: Making a presentation*

*Beginning a presentation*

◇ *Greeting and Introducing*: Good afternoon, everyone. Let me introduce myself. My name is James Lee, and I work as a salesperson (1) _____ the ABC Corporation.

◇ *Purpose*: The aim/subject of my talk is (2) _____ give you some information about the product we can offer you.

◇ *Structure*: I'm going to (3) _____ three points. First, I will talk about the product's features. Then I will tell you about its functions. (4) _____ , I will come to the benefits of the product.

*During a presentation*

◇ *First point*: I'd like to start with the features of our product.

◇ *Second point*: Well, that's all for the features. Now I'll (5) _____ on to the second point: the functions.

◇ *Third point*: That's all for the second point. My third point is (6) _____ the benefits of our product.

*Ending a presentation*

◇ *Conclusion*: In conclusion /In a word, I have (7) _____ three main points in my presentation. They are the features, functions and benefits of the product.

◇ *Answer questions*: If you have any questions, I'd be pleased/happy to (8) _____ them now.

◇ *Thanking*: I will stop here. I hope this has given you an idea of our product. Thank you for your (9) _____ /time.

## Task Two: Describing a trend

◇ The number increased (1) _____ 4,500 to 5 million.
◇ There was an increase in the (2) _____ from 4,500 to 5 million.
◇ The number dropped from 4,500 to 3,000.
◇ There was a (3) _____ in the number from 4,500 to 3,000.

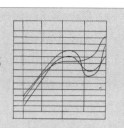

## Task Three: Demonstrating a product

◇ What are the (1) _____ of this product?
◇ What are the (2) _____ of this product?
◇ What are the (3) _____ of this product?
◇ What are the (4) _____ of this product?

## D Controlled practice

You are a salesperson, and your partner is a client. Make a sales presentation according to the following prompts. Listen to the recording of a model answer, and then follow it.

| | |
|---|---|
| Opening | ◇ Greeting.<br>◇ Introducing yourself: Patrick Wang from ADC.<br>◇ The aim: introduce ADC's security services.<br>◇ 3 main points: price, range of services and quality. |
| Point 1: | ◇ *Price:* At the moment, the client spends 1,500 pounds a month on security. ADC's price is 20% less for the same service. |
| Point 2: | ◇ *Range of services:* At the moment, the client is working with 3 different companies. ADC can provide all the services. |
| Point 3: | ◇ *Quality:* ADC was elected as number one security firm in this region. |
| Ending | ◇ In conclusion: a lower price, simpler administration and good quality.<br>◇ Thank the audience.<br>◇ Invite questions. |

## E Business culture

Work with your partner to answer the following questions. Then listen to the recording, and fill in the blanks.

(1) Have you ever made a business presentation? If you have, what was it about?
(2) How should you prepare a business presentation?
(3) What should you pay attention to during a presentation?

### Three P's for Presentations: Plan, Prepare and Practice

*Plan what you're going to say:*
Write the (1) _____ of your talk. Find out what your (2) _____ _____ are and write them down. Find out about your audience(听众): who are they? (3) _____ _____ of them will be there? What do they know about you and (4) _____ _____? What do they expect? Are they interested in your topic?

*Prepare your talk:*
Write the presentation out (5) _____ _____. Then take out the main points and put them on note cards. Use large (6) _____ _____ so that you can read your notes easily. (7) _____ the cards clearly.

Are you going to use visual aids(视觉辅助设备): projector, computer, and whiteboard? If so, prepare everything (8) _____ _____. Test the equipment before the talk and make sure everything (9) _____ properly.

Anticipate(预料) the questions you may be asked. Prepare answers to them. Make your answer (10) _____ _____ _____ _____ for the audience to understand.

*Practice giving a presentation:*
You may (11) _____ _____ a presentation in front of your friends or colleagues. They can ask you questions and (12) _____ you some (13) _____ on your talk and your body language. If possible, ask your friends to make a (14) _____ of your presentation.

When you are practicing, don't read your notes. You can refer to your notes while talking. And also remember to put passion into your talk. If you have no passion, audience will be bored.

## Part 2  Business Speaking

### A  Pair work

**Task One:** Work in pairs to practice using the expressions for opening a presentation. One of you asks the questions on the left, and the other provides a proper reply. The first one has been done as an example for you. After this practice, change the roles.

A: What is the expression for greeting the audience in an informal situation?

B: Morning, everyone.

A: What is the expression for greeting the audience in a formal situation?

B:

A: What is the expression for introducing the presentation topic?

B:

A: What is the expression for structuring your talk?

B:

*Task Two:* Work in pairs to practice using the expressions for opening a presentation. One of you asks the questions on the left, and the other provides a proper reply. After this practice, change the roles.

A: What is the expression for summarizing your presentation?

B:

A: What is the expression for saying when you are ready for questions?

B:

A: What is the expression for closing your presentation?

B:

A: What is the expression for thanking the audience?

B:

## B Role play

*Task One:* Make a mini presentation on "*How to make a good presentation*" according to the table below.

| Topic: | How to make a good presentation | |
|---|---|---|
| Opening: | (1) Introduce yourself. <br> (2) Introduce your topic: how to make a good presentation. <br> (3) Make three points: tips for opening, delivering the body, and ending. | |
| Point 1: | Tips for opening | ◇ Get the audience's attention. <br> ◇ Keep it short and simple. <br> ◇ Make a good first impression. |
| Point 2: | Tips for delivering the body | ◇ Put passion into your talk. <br> ◇ Maintain eye contact and look friendly. <br> ◇ Keep to your structure. |

续表

| | | |
|---|---|---|
| Point 3: | Tips for ending | ◇ Give a clear and short summary.<br>◇ Thank your audience and invite questions.<br>◇ Be polite with all questioners, even if they ask difficult questions. |
| Ending: | | (1) Summarize 3 points.<br>(2) Invite and answer questions.<br>(3) Thank the audience. |

*Task Two:* Work in small groups. Discuss with your partners and prepare a short talk on one of the topics below. Then take turns to deliver the talk.

(1) Why are there so many people studying English?
(2) Why is it so difficult to improve English?
(3) Why is it so difficult for a fresh graduate to get a good job?
(4) Why does campus love often fail?
(5) Why do women live longer than men?
(6) Why are there so many Chinese ladies marrying Westerners?

# Part 3  Listening Practice

## A Listening focus

**Diagrams (graphs, charts, tables)**

*Task One:* Listen to the passage twice and finish the diagram with the information you hear.

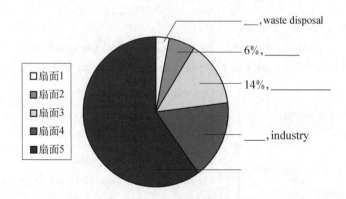

Unit 7

*Task Two:* Look at the charts below. They show the share price for eight different companies during a month. You will hear five sentences to describe 5 charts. Listen carefully and decide which chart each sentence describes.

(1) _____   (2) _____   (3) _____   (4) _____   (5) _____

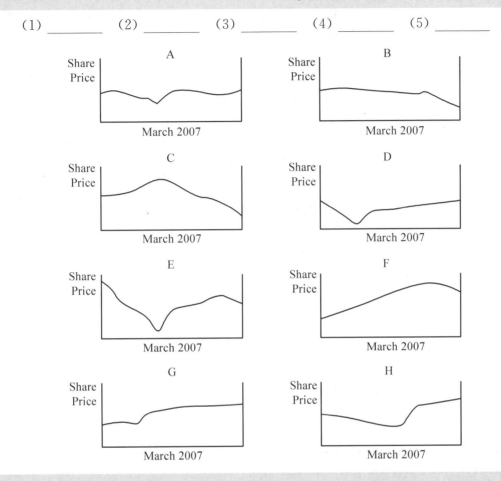

*Task Three:* Listen to four students talking about their future plans. As you listen, fill in the table with what you hear.

|  | What do they want to be in future? | What are they doing/going to do now? |
|---|---|---|
| Speaker 1 | _____ . | _____ . |
| Speaker 2 | _____ for a women's magazine. | _____ . |
| Speaker 3 | _____ . | _____ . |
| Speaker 4 | _____ . | _____ and making a lot of videos in his free time. |

# B Dictation

*Task One:* Listen to the short passage twice and fill in the blanks with the missing words or sentences.

CBE | 91

One of the most (1) _____ people make when discussing their product or service is to use the same type of (2) _____ again and again. They say the same thing in every presentation and hope that something in their presentation will attract the prospective customer. I have been a (3) _____ to this approach for many times when I could (4) _____ but listen to "canned" PowerPoint presentations.

(5) _____; change it slightly to include specific points that are (6) _____ to that particular customer. If you use PowerPoint, place the company's logo on your slides and describe how the key slides relate to their situation. (7) _____. This means that it is very important to ask your prospective customers probing questions before you start (8) _____ your company.

*Task Two:* You're going to hear five sentences. Repeat each sentence you hear. Then listen again and write down each sentence. Check your answer when you listen for the third time.

(1) _____
(2) _____
(3) _____
(4) _____
(5) _____

## ⓒ Conversations

**Conversation 1**

*Task One:* Mary has written down what Brown has suggested to her, but mainly by key words. Choose the proper key words to complete the statements.

| Key words: | | |
|---|---|---|
| A. animated and energetic | B. long-winded | C. busy |
| D. enthusiasm | E. boring and unimaginative | F. connection |

(1) First, you should create a _____ between your product and the prospect.
(2) Today's businesses are too _____ to listen to _____ discussions.
(3) The majority of the presentations I have heard have been _____, causing people to quickly lose interest in the presentation.
(4) When you discuss solutions, do you become more _____?
(5) Does your body language exhibit your _____?

*Task Two:* Listen to the conversation again and decide whether the following statements are true (T) or false (F).

(1) Try to avoid mentioning your competitors' products in a presentation.    (    )

(2) Know what your key points are and learn how to make them quickly. ( )
(3) The man is satisfied with most of the sales presentations he has heard. ( )
(4) A presentation should be full of energy and enthusiasm. ( )
(5) Proper body language can help you with the presentation. ( )

**Conversation 2**

*Task One:* Listen to the conversation and then rearrange the following steps according to the conversation.

(1) Look at individual members of your audience.
(2) Make sure you know how to pronounce the words in your presentation.
(3) Use natural gestures.
(4) Check that everyone can see you and your visual aids.
(5) Change the seating arrangement if you don't like it.
(6) Arrange your papers on the desk.
(7) Put your bag and notes in a suitable place.

The correct order should be:
_____ → _____ → _____ → _____ → _____ → _____ → _____

*Task Two:* Listen to the conversation again and choose the best answer.

(1) The conversation is mainly about the _____ of presentation.
　　A. preparation　　B. objective　　C. enthusiasm　　D. delivery skills
(2) Which of the following is NOT mentioned as a suggestion?
　　A. Turn off your mobile phone.
　　B. Proper position of bags and notes.
　　C. Make the seating arrangement comfortable for you.
　　D. Check the visual aids.
(3) By using natural gestures, the speaker means you should _____.
　　A. feel like an actor
　　B. act as if you were talking to a colleague
　　C. behave like a teacher speaking to students
　　D. look as if there's no audience at all
(4) In the eye-contact part, you should avoid _____.
　　A. staring at your audience
　　B. burying your head in your notes
　　C. any reference to your notes
　　D. conversational manners

(5) What should you do if there are words that are both used in English and in Chinese?
   A. Pronounce them in Chinese.
   B. Skip them in my presentation.
   C. Make sure how to pronounce them beforehand.
   D. Pronounce them in a Chinglish(Chinese-English) way.

## D Passage

*Task One:* Listen to the passage and group the suggestions in the right column under the categories specified in the left column. For example: suggestion No. 1 in the right column should be grouped under the topic concerning *speech*.

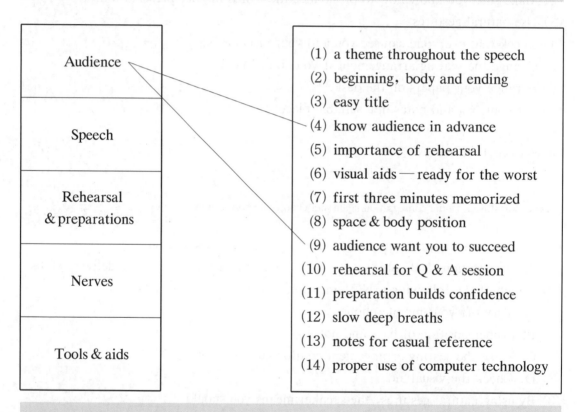

*Task Two:* Listen to the passage again. The following are some wrong ideas about a presentation. Correct the mistakes by quoting the suggestions from the passage. You may express them in your own words.

(1) I need a title that tells as much about my product as possible.
   Correct: _____
(2) Don't take your audience into consideration before you actually see them in your presentation.
   Correct: _____
(3) Visual aids will most likely go smoothly as in the rehearsal.

Correct: _____
(4) Question and answer session cannot be rehearsed.
Correct: _____
(5) The three Ps are planning, preparation and presentation.
Correct: _____

## Part 4  Fun Listening

*Task One:* Listen to the joke and decide whether the following statements are true (T) or false (F).

(1) The factory owner's visit had been announced before he came.   (   )
(2) The factory owner asked about the young man's salary simply because he was curious.   (   )
(3) The factory owner gave the young man $300.   (   )
(4) The boy lost his job.   (   )
(5) The boy benefited from this experience.   (   )

*Task Two:* A paradox is a seemingly contradictory statement that may nonetheless be true. Listen to the following sentences, each with a paradox in it, then complete them, by selecting the right words from the box below. Read them again and try to understand.

We have bigger houses and smaller _____.
We have conquered outer space but not _____ space.
We _____ more, but accomplish less.
We have higher _____ but lower morals.
We have more kinds of food, but less _____.

> incomes, plan, nutrition, families, inner

# Unit 8  Would you like to visit our factory

## Unit Goals
◇ Showing someone around the factory and answering questions
◇ Describing the production process
◇ Knowing about production process
◇ Understanding three main types of production process
◇ Understanding five steps for opening and ending a first business talk

## Part 1  Practical Listening & Speaking

### A  Word study

Work with your partner to fill in the blanks using the words on the left. Listen and check your answers, and then follow the recording.

| workshops |
| work shifts |
| Output |
| Granule |
| capacity |
| production line |
| malfunctions |
| inspection |
| turn...out |
| dispatch |

(1) If workers in a factory _____ _____, they work for a particular period of time, and are then replaced by others.

(2) When we _____ something _____, we produce or make it.

(3) Generally, _____ _____ is the same as assembly line.

(4) When we _____ something, we send it somewhere for a particular purpose.

(5) "How will you _____ your goods?" "We use plastic bags."

(6) When we _____ something, we attach a label onto it or write information on it.

(7) The food will stay fresh for longer because it is _____.

(8) When food is _____, it is preserved by putting into a metal container from which all the air is removed.

(9) When a machine _____, it's not working properly.

(10) However, on closer _____, a number of problems came up.

96

| canned |
| vacuum-sealed |
| label |
| package |

(11) _____ is the amount of work, goods, or people that are dealt with in a particular period of time.

(12) _____ is a small hard piece of something.

(13) We are now running at 100% of our _____.

(14) How many _____ do you have?

## B Functional listening

*Task One (Showing someone around the factory and answering questions)*: Listen to the recording and fill in the blanks.

Jane: This way please. We have two workshops. This is one of them. We have another one on the second floor.

Jack: It looks (1) _____. How big is it?

Jane: It's 30 meters x 40 meters.

Jack: How many people are there in this workshop?

Jane: There are 200 people, and they work shifts.

Jack: Can you tell me (2) _____?

Jane: Sure. We can produce 44 units per hour.

Jack: Then what's your weekly output?

Jane: The weekly output is 25,000 units, but it can be increased because we are now running only at 80% of our capacity.

Jack: Can you tell me (3) _____ in this production line?

Jane: Sure. Its performance is excellent, and it rarely malfunctions. It was imported from Germany.

Jack: What's the (4) _____?

Jane: We run our machine at 160 hours per week.

Jack: What about quality control? Do you have an inspection system?

Jane: Yes, of course. We have (5) _____ the whole production process so that no faulty goods will be turned out.

Jack: Can I have a look at your warehouse?

Jane: Certainly. This way, please. This is our warehouse.

Jack: Yes, it's very nice. (6) _____ I have a look at your control room?

Jane: I'm sorry. I'm afraid you can't. That one is not

open to visitors.

**Task Two** (*Describing the production process*): Listen to the recording and complete the following description of the steps in the production process of a potato supplier. Use the passive form.

The potatoes are (1) _____ on our farms and (2) _____ here to our new production plant. Firstly they are (3) _____, next they are (4) _____, and after that they are (5) _____, (6) _____, and (7) _____. Once they are "cooked", they are (8) _____ and (9) _____. Following that the granules are (10) _____ and vacuum-sealed. Finally the cans are labeled, packaged and dispatched.

## ⓒ Language check

Work with your partner to complete the following conversations. Then listen and check your answers.

**Task One: Showing someone around the factory and answering questions**

*Talking about workshops*

F: How many workshops do you have?
M: We have two workshops. One of them is on the first floor. The other one is on the second floor.
F: How (1) _____ is your workshop?
M: Each workshop has 410,000 (2) _____ feet of floor space.

*Talking about workers*

F: How many people are there in this plant?
M: We (3) _____ 500 workers, and they work shifts.

*Talking about the machine*

F: Can you tell me something about your machines?
M: Sure. All of our machines were (4) _____ from Germany. Their performance is excellent, and they seldom malfunction.
F: What's the weekly machine (5) _____ _____?
M: We run our machine at 150 hours per week.

*Talking about the output*

F: What is your output per hour?
M: We can (6) _____ 100 units per hour.

Unit 8

F: What's your weekly output?
M: Our weekly output is 15,000 units, but it (7) _____ be increased because we are now running only (8) _____ 80% of our capacity.

*Talking about quality control*

F: Do you have an inspection system?
M: Yes, of course. We have a (9) _____ of specialists to supervise the whole production process so that no faulty goods will be turned out.

*Asking to visit the warehouse or other places*

F: Can I have a look at your warehouse?
M: Certainly. This way, please. This is our warehouse.
F: Yes, it's very big. Do you mind if I have a look at your (10) _____ room?
M: I'm sorry. I'm afraid you can't. That one is not (11) _____ to visitors.

*Task Two: Describing the production process*

F: Could you tell me how the product is made?
M: Sure. The potatoes are grown on our farms and brought to our new production plant here. (1) _____ they are peeled, next they are washed, and (2) _____ _____ they are sorted, graded, and steamed. (3) _____ they are "cooked", they are chopped and freeze-dried. (4) _____ that the granules are canned and vacuum-sealed. Finally the cans are (5) _____, packaged and dispatched.

## D Controlled practice

Describe the production process of chocolate products based on the following table. Use the passive form. Listen to the recording of a model answer, and then follow it.

| |
|---|
| Buy cocoa beans from Malaysia and Ghana. |
| Sort, clean and roast cocoa beans. |
| Break cocoa beans into small pieces and blow away the shells. |
| Grind the small pieces and make mass. |
| Come to the actual chocolate-making process. |

## E Business culture

Work with your partner to answer the following questions. Then listen to the recording and fill in the blanks.

(1) Do you know how to open a business talk? What should you say to start a business conversation?
(2) In terms of body language (在身体语言方面), what should you pay attention to?
(3) What should you do to end a business conversation?

---

**Five Steps for Opening and Ending the First Business Talk**

When you first meet your business partner, you should open and end the business conversation appropriately. The following are some (1) _____ for you to make a successful first conversation in the workplace.

*Five steps for opening the talk*

◇ *Greeting and be welcoming:* You should first greet the visitor appropriately, and remember to say "Welcome to our company!" Also (2) _____ eye contact with the person in the talk.
◇ *Having proper handshake:* Smile and always (3) _____ _____ when you meet the visitor. Your handshake should be short and a bit tight. Beware of your other body language. Nervous people make others feel (4) _____. Look confident and comfortable.
◇ *Making introductions:* Take your time during introductions. You should introduce yourself and your (5) _____ to the visitor. Remember the visitor's name, and use it (6) _____ in the conversation.
◇ *Exchanging name cards:* Get your business card ready. Present it to the visitor using both hands. When you receive a business card from the visitor, you should put it in an (7) _____ _____. Don't put it in your trousers' pocket or your wallet.
◇ *Have proper small talk:* Be prepared for (8) _____ _____. Think of three topics you can talk about. For example, you may ask about the visitor's trip, talk about the (9) _____ _____, or ask about the visitor's hotel arrangement. Avoid all personal questions unless you know the person well.

*Five steps for ending the talk*
◇ Say you will follow up(跟进) or take action and (10) _____ _____ to the visitor as soon as possible.
◇ Thank the visitor for taking the time to visit you and say you really (11) _____ it.
◇ Say it was a (12) _____ to talk to (meet) the visitor, and say you are looking forward to seeing him/her again soon.
◇ Extend your hand and have an appropriate handshake with the person. Look at the eyes of the other person when shaking hands.
◇ Escort(护送) clients out and say goodbye.

# Part 2　Business Speaking

## A Pair work

*Task One:* Work in pairs. Change the following sentences to the passive form. The first one has been done for you as an example. Then take turns to read the sentences.

(1) We export the goods to Asia.
(2) The company manufactures the goods in Shanghai.
(3) They transport the raw materials by rail.
(4) We buy in (大量购买) the components(元件).
(5) He inspects the parts regularly.
(6) They dispose of the scrap (废料) right away.
(7) The workers assemble (装配) the instruments on the shop floor(车间).
(8) They package the finished products by hand.
(9) We repair the machine tools(机床) frequently.

A. The goods are exported to Asia.
B.
C.
D.
E.
F.
G.
H.
I.

*Task Two:* Work in pairs. Use the comparative form to complete the following sentences. The first one has been done for you as an example. Then take turns to read the sentences.

(1) With the new system, output is higher and costs are lower.

(2) The conventional machines are _____ but the new ones are _____.

(3) I think this scheduling plan is _____, and it is _____ to implement.

(4) Our latest product is _____, _____, and _____.

(5) We are trying to make our distribution network _____ and _____.

(6) Robots make material handling _____.

(7) The new machine tools are not only _____ but _____ and _____.

(8) Although our traditional products are _____, they are still _____ with customers.

(9) The workers are _____ in the _____, _____ production shed (厂房).

## B Role play

*Task One:* You are a machine operator. Your partner is a machine supplier's representative. You have difficulty understanding the instructions on the left. Your partner "translates" them into more conversational English on the right. First match each difficult term with its conversational translation. Then practice a dialogue.

A: First, remove the cover.
B: I'm sorry. I don't understand.
A: In other words, take off the cover.
B: Oh, I see.

(1) Connect the device to the power source.

(2) Place the laser-camera in the portable (手提式) container provided.

(3) Replace the cover.

(4) Introduce the cartridge.

(5) Ensure that the alarm system is fully operational.

(6) Insert the electronic key.

(7) Remove the unit from the protective packaging.

(8) Withdraw the card from the slot (插卡处).

(9) Reset the dial to zero.

(10) Enter the code number on the keyboard.

(11) Select the appropriate switch setting.

A. Turn the dial back to "0".

B. Make sure the alarm is working properly.

C. Put in the electronic key.

D. Take the card out.

E. Put the cover back.

F. Unpack (打开包裹) the unit.

G. Put the cartridge (墨盒) in.

H. Choose the right setting.

I. Punch in (输入) the code.

J. Put the camera in its carrying-case.

K. Plug in the apparatus (器械).

Unit 8

***Task Two:*** Look at the pictures in the following table, which are about some basic production activities. Then take turns to describe the activities.

A: Can you describe your production process?
B: Sure. First, we design our products. Then...

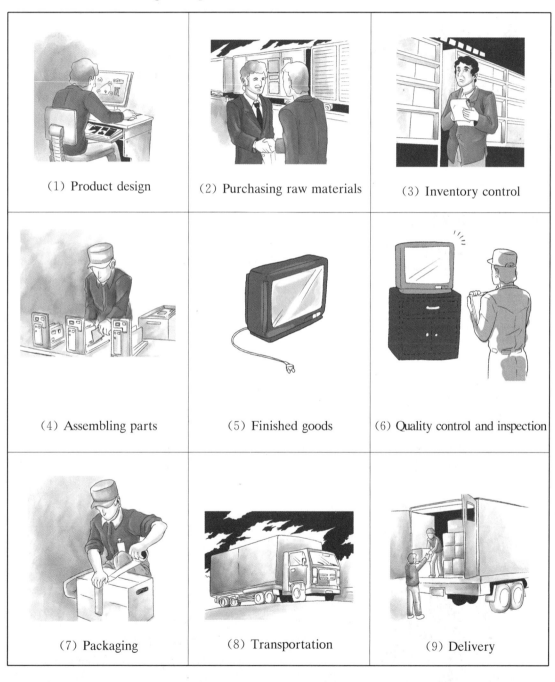

***Task Three:*** Various kinds of problems may occur in the production process. The following are the common ones. Work with your partner to solve them.

A: The machine is out of order again. What can we do?
B: I think we should call the maintenance engineer without delay.

| | |
|---|---|
| Processes | ◇ Bottleneck (too many things stuck in the system)<br>◇ Stoppage (the system has to stop)<br>◇ Shutdown (the system or factory has to close) |
| Machines | ◇ Suffering from wear and tear (damage from use)<br>◇ Out of order (not working)<br>◇ Out of commission (not usable at the moment) |
| Products | ◇ Damaged (broken)<br>◇ Defective (faulty) or flawed (not perfect)<br>◇ Substandard (not as good as usual) |
| People | ◇ Strikes (workers refusing to work)<br>◇ Go-slows (working too slowly)<br>◇ Disputes (disagreements with bosses)<br>◇ Absenteeism (workers staying away from work) |

# Part 3 Listening Practice

## A Listening focus

**Following instructions (process, steps)**

*Task One:* You will hear the instruction for making salad. Listen carefully and put the following expressions in right order by writing the numbers next to them.

_____ First you wash the lettuce and cut it up.
_____ Now peel some potatoes.
_____ After that you prepare the mushrooms.
_____ Then you slice a cucumber.
_____ Next you chop up a carrot.
_____ Slice some onions.
_____ Then you slice some tomatoes.
_____ Finally you mix all the ingredients together.

*Task Two:* Listen to a letter carefully and match each sentence in Column A with that in Column B. For No. 6 complete the information in Column B.

| Column A | Column B |
| --- | --- |
| (1) If school is in session, | A. contact your supervisor immediately and complete an incident report form. |
| (2) If you are injured during hours when the nurse is not on duty, | B. the employee must present a medical provider card (given out by the school nurse) and complete an Initial Medical Treatment Report form. |
| (3) If the injury is of an emergent nature, | C. report to the school nurse to receive initial medical treatment and complete an incident report form. |
| (4) When seeking medical treatment from a provider for approved worker's compensation claims, | D. all follow-up appointments will be scheduled around the employee's work hours. |
| (5) Once the employee is medically cleared to return to work, | E. go immediately to the nearest hospital emergency room for treatment. |
| (6) If there is any question, please contact | _____. |

## B Dictation

*Task One:* Listen to the short passage twice and fill in the blanks with the missing words or sentences.

The production process is concerned with transforming a range of inputs into those outputs that are required by the market. This (1) _____ two main sets of resources: the transforming resources, and the transformed resources.

The transforming resources include the buildings, machinery, computers, and people that (2) _____ the transforming processes. The transformed resources are the (3) _____ and components that are transformed into (4) _____.

Any production process involves a series of links in a production chain. (5) _____. Adding value involves making a product more desirable to a consumer so that (6) _____. Adding value therefore is not just about manufacturing, but (7) _____ all processes e. g. advertising, promotion, distribution, etc. that make the final product more desirable.

It is very important for businesses to (8) _____ the processes that add value, so that they can enhance these processes to the ongoing benefit of the business.

*Task Two:* You're going to hear five sentences. Repeat each sentence you hear. Then listen again and write down each sentence. Check your answer when you listen for the third time.

(1) _____
(2) _____
(3) _____
(4) _____
(5) _____

## C Conversations

**Conversation 1**

*Task One:* Listen to the conversation and fill in the missing information.

| Farmers | At the _____ of the production chain | | |
|---|---|---|---|
| We | cleaning | ensure materials such as _____ and _____ are removed | |
| | isolated | | |
| | _____ | _____ | |
| | heated (between _____ ℃ and _____ ℃ for 20 to 50 minutes) | | |

Unit 8 Would you like to visit our factory

**Task Two:** Listen to the conversation again, and then choose the best answer.

(1) What are they visiting?
   A. A farm.                     B. A chocolate factory.
   C. A coffee house.             D. A bakery.
(2) At which stage are the shells cracked open?
   A. The start of production chain.    B. Cleaning.
   C. Winnowing.                        D. Heating.
(3) Which statement is true about winnowing?
   A. It's all done by machine.
   B. It is done before cleaning.
   C. Farmers play an important role in it.
   D. It's the end of the production chain.
(4) Why is there a temperature and time limit for roasting beans?
   A. Only in this way can the shells be cracked.
   B. To release the cocoa's full flavour and aroma.
   C. To remove the unnecessary parts from the beans.
   D. To make the work easy for farmers.
(5) From this conversation, we learn that _____.
   A. their products are only sold in domestic market
   B. the cleaning stage is fully automatic without workers
   C. they burn the furnace by gas
   D. the visitor thinks highly of their products

**Conversation 2**

*Task One:* Listen to the conversation and fill in the chart with the missing information.

Chart One:

Chart Two:

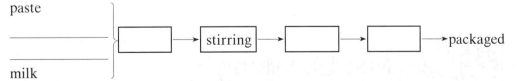

*Task Two:* Listen to the conversation again and match the name of each stage on the left with the explanation on the right.

(1) grinding      A. combines varieties of cocoa paste to ensure a consistent final product
(2) blending      B. at 45℃ to produce an even smoother end product
(3) refining      C. shapes the chocolate
(4) stirring      D. reduces the size of the particles
(5) heating      E. breaks down the cocoa butter on the beans and produces a smooth liquid
(6) molding      F. produces a smooth and glossy chocolate

## D Passage

*Task One:* Listen to the passage and decide whether the following statements are true (T) or false (F).

(1) A number of identical units can be produced in parallel under job production.　　　　　　　　　　　　　　　　　　　　　　　　　　　　　　　( )
(2) One worker may carry out two jobs at the same time in job production. ( )
(3) Batch production is sometimes referred to as "intermittent" production. ( )
(4) Batch production is characterized by regularity. ( )
(5) In flow production, units go from one stage to the next without stopping or waiting.
　　　　　　　　　　　　　　　　　　　　　　　　　　　　　　　　　　　　( )

*Task Two:* Listen to the passage again and match the statements on the right with the type of production on the left.

| Type of production | Statements |
|---|---|
| Job production ____ , ____ | (1) It is unique in the fact that the project is considered to be a single operation. |
| | (2) Different job types are held as work-in-progress between the various stages of production. |
| Batch production ____ , ____ | (3) The project requires the complete attention of the worker before he or she passes on to the next job. |
| | (4) A continuous process of parts and sub-assemblies passes on from one stage to another until completion. |
| Flow production ____ | (5) A group of components go through a production process together. As one group finishes, the next one starts. |

## Part 4   Fun Listening

*Task One:* Listen to a study on the American Male's Recreational Preferences and complete the table.

| For unemployed or imprisoned people | basketball |
|---|---|
| For maintenance level employees | _____ |
| For _____ | football |
| For supervisors | baseball |
| For _____ | tennis |
| For corporate officers | _____ |

***Task Two:*** Choose the best answer to the following question.

What conclusion does the National Science Foundation draw?

The conclusion is: The higher you rise in the corporate structure, _____.

A. the smaller your boss becomes

B. the more similar your balls become

C. the smaller your balls become

D. the more similar your boss becomes

# Unit 9  This is our lowest price

## Unit Goals

- Negotiating prices and discounts
- Negotiating terms of payment
- Developing relationships first or doing business first
- Following instructions while listening
- Applying skills of a good salesperson

## Part 1  Practical Listening & Speaking

### A  Word study

Work with your partner to fill in the blanks using the words on the left. Listen and check your answers, and then follow the recording.

|  |  |
|---|---|
| wholesale price<br>unacceptable<br>unit price<br>quote<br>competitive<br>superior<br>reduce the price<br>size of your order<br>profit margin<br>terms of payment<br>offer | (1) We would like to pay by _____ _____ _____ _____.<br>(2) Could you _____ us a large discount?<br>(3) Could you _____ us your lowest price?<br>(4) Unless you _____ _____ _____, business is rather impossible.<br>(5) How long is your _____ _____? When is the deadline for payment?<br>(6) As this is our first _____, we would like you to pay by L/C.<br>(7) Our _____ _____ is $300. That's to say, the price is charged for selling goods in large quantities.<br>(8) Our _____ _____ is $350. That's to say, the price is charged for each single item that is sold.<br>(9) Your price is completely _____. That's too high.<br>(10) Our price is very _____. We provide a high standard of service at a very reasonable price.<br>(11) Our products are of _____ quality. |

| an irrevocable documentary L/C |
|---|
| transaction |
| credit period |

(12) Our discount depends on the _____ _____ _____ _____ _____. If your order is a large one, you will enjoy a large discount.

(13) We have a very small _____ _____. We can't make much money.

(14) What are your _____ _____ _____?

## B Functional listening

*Task One (Negotiating prices and discounts):* Listen to the recording and fill in the blanks.

Rita: So what's the unit price?

Jack: Our standard unit price to the wholesaler is $24.

Rita: I'm afraid that (1) _____.
This is not a standard situation.

Jack: Yes, I know that. If you buy 30,000 units, I can offer a unit price of $22.

Rita: Your price is too high. I'm afraid (2) _____. Otherwise it's difficult for us to continue the talk. Could you please quote us your lowest price?

Jack: Our price has already been at its lowest level, and it's very competitive. Please also note that our (3) _____ quality.

Rita: Unless you can reduce the price, I'm afraid business is rather impossible.

Jack: Let's talk about discount rather than unit price. If you order 30,000 units, I can (4) _____.

Rita: I'm afraid 5% is not acceptable. I'm looking for a large discount, and I hope you're going to allow me one.

Jack: Our discount depends on the size of buyers' order. If you want a big discount, then you (5) _____ a big one.

Rita: Could you offer us a 10% discount on 35,000 units?

Jack: I'm afraid that's not possible. With 10% discount, we will have no profit margin at all. (6) _____ on 35,000 units?

Rita: I'm afraid that's not acceptable. 8% on 35,000 units. This is my last offer. Take it or leave it.
Jack: I think that offer will be acceptable.

> *Task Two (Negotiating terms of payment)*: Listen to the conversation and complete the following notes using one or two words from the recording.

(1) The man prefers an irrevocable documentary L/C for the _____ _____.
(2) According to the woman's company policy, the payment is within 30 days of _____.
(3) In the end, they have reached an agreement on a 60-day _____ _____.
(4) They have also agreed that a discount of _____ will be offered on _____ units.

## C  Language check

> Work with your partner to complete the following conversations, and then listen and check your answers.

### Task One: Negotiating prices and discounts

*Asking about the unit price*

M: What's the unit (retail) price? (Can you tell me the unit price?)
F: Our unit price (1) _____ the wholesaler is $23.

*Asking for a lower price*

M: I'm afraid that your price is completely unacceptable. Could you (2) _____ (bring down/reduce) your price?
F: I think our price is very reasonable. How about $21?

*Asking for the lowest price*

M: I'm afraid it's still too (3) _____. Unless you can reduce the price, I'm afraid business is rather impossible. Could you please (4) _____ us your lowest price?
F: Our price is at its lowest level and it's very competitive. Please also note that our product is of (5) _____ quality.

*Asking for the discount*

M: Quality must be good; otherwise I won't order. Let's talk about the (6) _____ rather than the unit price. Can you offer us a good discount?

F: How about 5% discount (7) _____ 30,000 units?

*Asking for the largest discount*

M: I'm afraid 5% is not acceptable. I'm looking for a large discount. What's your largest discount?

F: Our discount (8) _____ _____ the size of buyers' order. If you want a big discount, then you must make the order a big one. Well, if you order 40,000 units, I can offer you a discount of 7%.

*Reaching an agreement*

M: I'm afraid that's not acceptable. Now this is my last (9) _____: 8% on 40,000 units. Take it or leave it.

F: I think that offer will be acceptable.

*Summarizing*

M: Let's clarify the (10) _____ so far. We've agreed on a 8% discount on 40,000 units. Is that right?

F: Yes, that's right.

**Task Two: Negotiating terms of payment**

*Asking about terms of payment*

M: What are your terms of payment?

F: We (1) _____ an irrevocable documentary L/C for the first transaction.

*Asking for other terms of payment*

M: Can you (2) _____ D/A?

F: I'm afraid we can't accept that.

*Asking about the credit period*

M: How (3) _____ is your credit period?

F: Our policy is payment within 30 days of delivery.

*Asking for a longer credit period*

M: I'm afraid that's not acceptable. How about 90 days?

F: 90 days! I'm sorry. I'm afraid that's not (4) _____.

*Reaching an agreement*

M: Can I just remind you that we are making a large order?

F: Yes, I know you're making a large order, but you are also getting an (5) _____ product (6) _____ a very large discount.
M: I know that, but your credit period is too short.
F: OK. How about 60 days?
M: That (7) _____ fair enough.

*Summarizing*

F: Let's clarify the position so far. We've agreed on a 60-day (8) _____ period. Is that correct?
M: Yes, that's correct.

**Task Three: Talking about quality**

◇ This is a quality product.
◇ Our products are (1) _____ for their superior quality.
◇ The material is absolutely (2) _____ excellent quality.
◇ Our goods are well (3) _____ in Asian market.

## D Controlled practice

You are a seller. Your partner is a buyer. Make a telephone conversation according to the following prompts. Listen to the recording of a model answer, and then follow it.

| YOU | YOUR PARTNER |
|---|---|
| Order 100 SDF machines — product number 453. | No problem! Ask when they are needed. |
| ASAP. Ask for 10% discount. | Refuse. Prices are already discounted. |
| Ask for unit price. | $ 100. |
| Offer $ 95. | Refuse. Suggest 2.5% discount if money is paid at the time of the order. |
| Refuse. Ask for 3.5% with 60 days to pay. | Refuse. Say margins are very tight. |
| Comment. Say you will call again tomorrow. You expect a better offer. | Your prices are very competitive. Say goodbye. |

# E Business culture

Work with your partner to answer the following questions. Then listen to the recording, and fill in the blanks.

(1) Do you think American business people come to business first or develop relationships first?
(2) Politeness and respect for old people is very important in Japanese and Chinese cultures. Do you think so?
(3) In China, relationships often come before business. Do you agree with it? Give an example if you agree.

*Relationships First or Business First*

In the world of business, the way of doing business varies from one culture to another. People in some cultures (1) _____ _____ to business first while those in others (2) _____ relationships first.

In the United States, managers like to be (3) _____ in business transactions. The expressions "Time is money" and "Let's get to the point" are part of the (4) _____ _____. So in the U.S.A., managers like direct discussions, including open disagreement and (5) _____ _____. In this culture, relationships are important, but business always comes first. People in this culture often say: "Let's get down to business first."

In Latin American countries, business people think relationships are very important. They often start (6) _____ _____ _____ each other instead of coming direct to business. So you should develop strong social relationships with people first. (7) _____ _____ in this culture often say: "Do business with individuals, not companies." In other words, (8) _____ like to do business with people they know and like, so making non-business (9) "_____ _____" during meetings and going to social events are very important.

In Japan, politeness and respect for age and rank are very important for good business relationships. Perhaps the most important thing to remember in Japan is never (10) _____ _____ with someone in a meeting. This can embarrass the other people and they will probably not trust you as a business partner.

In China, relationships often come before business. Chinese business people often develop relationships first before coming to (11) _____ _____ because they believe a good relationship is very important for reaching agreements and also for (12) _____ _____. In order to develop good relationships, they often invite their business partners to dinner or invite them to go sightseeing. It's not surprising that lots of important agreements are reached (13) _____ _____.

# Part 2  Business Speaking

# A Pair work

*Task One:* Work in pairs. Learn to ask questions using the information on the left. The first one has been done as an example for you. After this practice, answer the questions on the right.

| | | |
|---|---|---|
| (1) Asking the unit price | A. What's your unit price? Can you tell me your unit price? |  |
| (2) Asking for a lower price | B. | |
| (3) Asking for the lowest price | C. | |
| (4) Asking for a large discount | D. | |
| (5) Asking for the largest discount | E. | |
| (6) Asking for terms of payment | F. | |

***Task Two:*** You are a seller. Your partner is a buyer. Make a dialogue according to the following table.

| | |
|---|---|
| Comment on the good quality of your product. | Agree. Ask for the unit price. |
| Quote your unit price ($35). | Say it's too high. Ask for a lower price. |
| Offer a lower price ($32). | Say it's still too high. Ask for the lowest price. |
| Say your price is already at its lowest level. | Ask for a large discount on 30,000 units. |
| Offer a 5% discount on 30,000 units. | Say it's too small. Ask for the largest one. |

| | |
|---|---|
| Say your discount depends on the order quantity. Offer a 7% discount on 35,000 units.<br><br>Agree. | Disagree. Ask for an 8% discount on 35,000 units.<br><br>Clarify the position. |

## B Role play

*Task One:* You are a builder (建筑商). Your partner is a supplier (供应商). Role-play a negotiation according to the following situations. After the practice, change roles.

*Information for you (builder)*

You are a builder and are looking for a supplier of windows for some offices you are building. This is what you want. When you have finished, fill in what you get.

| | You want | You get |
|---|---|---|
| Unit price: | $ 500 | |
| Discount: | 10% | |
| Credit period: | 60 days | |
| Delivery: | In 2 weeks | |
| Warranty: | 2 years | |

*Information for your partner (supplier)*

You are a supplier of windows. This is what you want. When you have finished, fill in what you get.

| | You want | You get |
|---|---|---|
| Unit price: | $ 1,000 | |
| Discount: | 0% | |
| Credit period: | 30 days | |
| Delivery: | In 6 weeks | |
| Warranty: | 6 months | |

***Task Two:*** The Irrevocable Letter of Credit（不可撤销信用证）is the most commonly used method of payment for imports. Exporters can be sure that they will be paid when they dispatch the goods, and importers have proof that the goods have been dispatched according to their instructions. Take turns to describe the Irrevocable Letter of Credit.

A: What is an Irrevocable Letter of Credit?
B: It's an inter-bank communication. The two banks take full responsibility that both shipment and payments are in order. Let me tell you the detailed operations.

(1) The importer and the exporter agree on a sales contract and the terms of the Documentary Credit.
(2) The importer asks their bank to open a Documentary Credit in the exporter's favor.
(3) The importer's bank（the issuing bank/开证行）sends a Letter of Credit to a bank in the exporter's country（the advising bank/通知行）.
(4) The exporter presents the shipping documents to the advising bank as proof that the shipment has been dispatched. If everything is in order, they are paid.
(5) The advising bank sends the documents to the issuing bank.
(6) The issuing bank sends the documents to the importer, who uses them to obtain delivery of the goods.

# Part 3　Listening Practice

## A Listening focus

### Weather Forecast

***Task One:*** Listen to the weather forecast and answer the following questions with what you hear.

(1) What will the weather be like in Seattle?
　_____

(2) What will the weather be like in Spokane?
　_____ during the day and _____ in the evening.

(3) What will the weather be like in the mountains?
　_____.

***Task Two:*** Listen to the weather forecast and fill in the table with what you hear.

|  | Weather features | Places |
|---|---|---|
| Today | _____ and a scattering of _____ | Scotland, N. Ireland and the far N. of England |
| | _____ with heavier showers, and prolonged thundery _____ | Elsewhere |
| | Dry | The far SE |
| Tonight | _____ with some clear intervals | the SE |
| | Showers | _____ |
| Thursday | _____, with the odd heavy one | _____ |
| | _____ | In the southwest |

## B Dictation

*Task One:* Listen to the short passage twice and fill in the blanks with the missing words or sentences.

Relationship marketing looks at customers and clients over a longer term. It (1) _____ the lifetime value of a customer.

Many experts think (2) _____, to find a new customer, as to sell to an (3) _____. With those financial realities in mind, the (4) _____ makes some sense, and some real dollars.

Relationship marketing is based on the idea that (5) _____ _____. After all, it's easier to buy from a friend, than from someone you've never heard of before. It's a matter of (6) _____.

It's said that people need to hear an offer at least seven times before they buy. That concept certainly works against the single step marketing method.

The (7) _____ buyers for your products and services begin to turn into (8) ____ _____ customers over time.

*Task Two:* You're going to hear five sentences. Repeat each sentence you hear. Then listen again and write down each sentence. Check your answer when you listen for the third time.

(1) _____

(2) _____

(3) _____

(4) _____

(5) _____

## ⓒ Conversations

**Conversation 1**

*Task One:* Listen to the conversation and choose the best answer to each question.

(1) What product or service is the telemarketer promoting?
   A. A special airfare discount.
   B. A membership to a sports club.
   C. A hotel in Hawaii.
   D. A subscription to a newspaper.

(2) Which special feature is NOT part of this offer?
   A. Access to free meals and beverages.
   B. Use of fitness rooms.
   C. Unrestricted use to a swimming pool.
   D. Introductory price is less than $ 40.

(3) Why does the man turn down the offer?
   A. He doesn't have extra money to spend.
   B. He never buys things over the phone.
   C. He doesn't need the service being provided.
   D. The telemarketer has called up before.

(4) Which statement is true about the "do not call" list according to the conversation?
   A. It will take four to six weeks to remove the man's name from the company's phone list.
   B. The man might be called by another company representative in the coming weeks.
   C. The man can request that his name be added again to the company's database.
   D. The man won't be called if his name is put on the list.

(5) What is the man's name?
   A. Mr. Phillips.    B. Mr. Jones.    C. Mr. Wendy.    D. Mr. Williams.

*Task Two:* Listen to the conversation again and decide whether the following statements are true (T) or false (F).

(1) The man received the call in the early morning. (　)

(2) The man has received similar calls occasionally. (　)

(3) It is free of charge to gain the membership to the sports club. (　)

(4) The man can enjoy all the facilities of the club if he pays $99.39. (   )
(5) The man turned down the offer as he had already accepted another offer. (   )
(6) It seems the man is tired of this kind of calling. (   )

**Conversation 2**

*Task One:* Listen to the conversation and choose the best answer to complete each statement.

(1) They have had a discussion on _____.
   A. payment, quality and quantity
   B. price, quality and quantity
   C. price, quality and payment
   D. payment, price and quality

(2) Mrs. Wang prefers D/A or D/P since _____.
   A. D/A or D/P is cheaper than letter of credit
   B. letter of credit takes longer time
   C. letter of credit will increase the cost of her imports
   D. D/A or D/P can reduce the cost of the imports

(3) Mr. Smith suggests that Mrs. Wang _____.
   A. discuss the payment with the bank
   B. have a talk over the deposit of a letter of credit with the bank
   C. reduce the bank charge related to the credit
   D. pay a deposit to the bank

(4) Mrs. Wang makes a suggestion that _____.
   A. goods be paid by D/A
   B. goods be paid by D/P
   C. 50% be paid by L/C and the rest by D/A
   D. 50% be paid by L/C and the balance by D/P

(5) At the end of the conversation, Mr. Smith and Mrs. Wang _____.
   A. disagree on the terms of payment
   B. accept the payment of letter of credit
   C. accept the payment of D/P
   D. cancel the business

*Task Two:* Listen to the conversation again and write down the features of a letter of credit.

Letter of credit:
√   increases _____
√   requires _____
√   will give the exporter _____

## D Passage

**Task One:** Listen to the passage and choose the best answer to each question.

(1) Why are buyers good actors?
   A. You are the only audience.
   B. You are the only person who has the products the buyer needs.
   C. They can perform.
   D. Though they need the products they act as if they will not buy it if 10% reduction is not offered.

(2) What does "Give me your best price" mean?
   A. "Give me the lowest price".
   B. "Give me the highest price".
   C. "Give me your best offer".
   D. "Give me the cheapest price".

(3) What usually happens if you give your best price?
   A. The business is done.
   B. A successive business will be done.
   C. The buyer wants more.
   D. The buyer is satisfied with the price.

(4) What will you do first if you want to drop the price by 10%?
   A. Tell the buyer you want to offer him a favorable price.
   B. Start out the reduction little by little.
   C. Start out with 2%.
   D. Tell the buyer 4% reduction is the bottom price.

(5) What might you get if you insist on your price?
   A. A failure in business.    B. Fruitful gains.
   C. A concession in business.    D. A discount offered.

**Task Two:** Listen to the passage again and apply the skills you have learned to the the following situations.

Situation 1
   Your customer insists on 10% reduction in price or he/she will go elsewhere.

_____

Situation 2
   You want to allow 10% reduction in price.

_____

## Part 4  Fun Listening

**Task One:** Listen to the tongue twister and try to follow it.

How much wood would a woodchuck chuck, if a woodchuck could chuck wood? He would chuck, he would, as much as he could. And chuck as much wood as a woodchuck would, if a woodchuck could chuck wood.

**Task Two:** Listen to the joke *Expensive Popcorn* and answer the question "Why is the popcorn more expensive than before?"

# Unit 10 What would you like to order

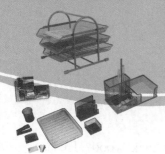

## Unit Goals

◇ Understanding how to place an order
◇ Tracking an order on the phone
◇ Improving your listening on the phone
◇ Guessing meanings while listening

## Part 1  Practical Listening & Speaking

### A Word study

Work with your partner to fill in the blanks using the words on the left. Listen and check your answers, and then follow the recording.

| |
|---|
| place an order for |
| account number |
| slash |
| deluxe model |
| total |
| helmet |
| fill an order |
| invoiced us |
| track an order |

(1) A _____ is a strong hard hat that soldiers, the police etc. wear to protect their heads.

(2) When you _____ _____ _____, you check the progress of it.

(3) When you _____ _____ _____, you supply the goods that a customer has ordered.

(4) When you _____ _____ _____, you supply the goods to a customer in the usual way.

(5) When you _____ _____ _____ of your order, you try to find out where it is.

(6) We'd like to order 100 boxes of _____ _____ _____.

(7) We'll send the goods to you by _____ _____.

(8) I'd like to _____ _____ _____ _____ some photocopiers.

(9) A _____ is a line (/) used in writing to separate numbers or letters.

Unit 10

> terracotta floor tiles
> check the status
> process an order
> forwarder
> sea freight

(10) A _____ is a company that makes money through sending letters or goods for others.

(11) A _____ _____ is of better quality and more expensive than other things of the same type.

(12) The company _____ _____ for the cost of using their conference room.

(13) That's £8,000 and £4,000, so the _____ is £12,000.

(14) Could you tell me your _____ _____?

## B Functional listening

*Task One (Placing an order on the phone):* Listen to the recording and fill in the blanks.

Alan: Good morning, Euro Bikes. How may I help you?

Stella: Good morning. This is Stella Chan from TNT Sports. I'd like to (1) _____ in your new catalogue.

Alan: Do you have an account with us, Ms. Chan?

Stella: Yes. The account number is MX56/890.

Alan: MX56/890. OK, what exactly would you like, Ms. Chan?

Stella: I'd like to order (2) _____ at $159 each, deluxe model. The item number is P21G5.

Alan: They're $159 each, so that's a total of $15,900. OK, what else would you like?

Stella: I'd like to order a hundred helmets. (3) _____.

Alan: So that's 100 helmets at $60 each. The total price is $6,000. Will that be all, Ms. Chan?

Stella: Yes. That's all for the moment.

Alan: OK. Could I just check your order, Ms. Chan?

Stella: Sure.

Alan: That's 100 mountain bikes — item number is P21G5. And there are also 100 helmets — item number is P2251. Without discount, (4) _____. But with our usual 15% discount, the price is $18,615. Is that correct?

Stella: Yes, that's correct.

Alan: Could you send us an email to confirm the order?
Stella: Yes, of course. We'll send it to you right away.
Alan: Thank you. We'll (5) _____ and invoice you as usual. Is that OK?
Stella: Yes, that will be fine.

> **Task Two (Tracking an order on the phone):** Listen to the recording and check (√) *True* or *False*.

|  | True | False |
|---|---|---|
| (1) Mr. Burton calls to check the progress of his order. | ☐ | ☐ |
| (2) His order number was IG345/893. | ☐ | ☐ |
| (3) His order was for four tiles. | ☐ | ☐ |
| (4) His order was sent to his forwarder before 20th August. | ☐ | ☐ |

## ❸ Language check

> Work with your partner to complete the following conversations, and then listen and check your answers.

### Task One: Placing an order on the phone

*Greeting and asking for the account number*

F: Good morning, ABC Corporation. How may I help you?
M: I'd like to place an order (1) _____ you for some office furniture.
F: Do you have an account with us, sir?
M: Yes. The account (2) _____ is MX567/900.

*Asking for order details*

F: What exactly would you like, sir?
M: I'd like to (3) _____ 100 executive chairs — item number is P3464.
F: 100 executive chairs. They're $115 (4) _____, so that's a total of $11,500. OK, what else would you like?
M: I'd like to order 50 deluxe desks at $350 each — item number is P4566.

*Checking the details*

F: OK. Could I just (5) _____ your order, please?
M: Sure.

126 ∎ Unit 10  *What would you like to order*

Unit 10

F: That's 100 executive chairs and 50 deluxe desks. Without discount, the total price is $29,000. But with our (6) _____ 25% discount, the price is $21,750. Is that correct?
M: Yes, that's correct.

*Asking for a confirmation and promising action*

F: Could you send us an (7) _____ to confirm the order?
M: Yes, of course. We'll send it to you right away.
F: Thank you. We'll carry (8) _____ your order as soon as possible.
M: Thank you.

**Task Two: Tracking an order on the phone**

*Greeting*

F: Good afternoon, MAT Corporation. How may I help you?
M: Hello, I'm trying to find (1) _____ if our order has been shipped. (Could I check the progress of our order, please?)

*Asking for order number*

F: Could I have your purchase (2) _____ number please?
M: Yes, it's BX456/788.

*Giving information*

F: Your order was shipped last night. You (3) _____ be able to receive it by the end of the month.
M: Great. Thank you.

**Task Three: Saying figures**

- I'm calling (1) _____ invoice NO. D/7745A5.
- Pre-tax profit is $32,345,678.
- The interest (2) _____ is 6.05% per annum.
- The next meeting is on the 2$^{nd}$ of October at 10:30.
- The (3) _____ exchange rate is $1.53 to the pound.
- The container measures 5.85 m × 2.35 m × 2.35 m.
- The Dow Jones was (4) _____ 44 points: a change of 1.25%.

## D Controlled practice

You are a supplier. Your partner is a buyer who places an order with you. Work together to make a telephone conversation based on the following prompts. Listen to the recording of a model answer, and then follow it.

| YOU | YOUR PARTNER |
|---|---|
| Greet. | Introduce yourself. Say you'd like to place an order. |
| Ask for the account number. | Give your account number: PJ/8723. |
| Ask for order details. | Order 20 fax machines — item number LQG/6701. |
| Ask anything else? | Say that's all. |
| Check the details: 20 fax machines at $ 450 each — item number LQG/6701. | Say that's correct. |
| Ask him to confirm by email or fax. | Say you will send a fax soon. |
| Promise action and thank the caller. | End the call. |

## E Business culture

Work with your partner to answer the following questions. Then listen to the recording, and fill in the blanks.

(1) Have you ever made an English phone call? Did you understand everything that was said?
(2) If you don't understand the other speaker very well, what are the reasons?
(3) How can you improve your listening on the phone?

---

**Improving Your Listening on the Phone**

*Reasons for not understanding:*
- The speaker talks too fast, too quietly or has an unfamiliar (1) _____ .
- He or she uses words that are new to you.
- You are discussing a (2) _____ which you do not know well.
- There is a lot of background noise.
- You lose your (3) _____ .
- You think you understand, but actually you don't. Later, there are problems.
- People (4) _____ each other or speak at the same time.
- The speaker organizes the information illogically (不符合逻辑地) or does not explain clearly.

*Strategies for dealing with difficulties in understanding:*

- Concentrate on the listening and stay (5) _____ _____.
- Prepare everything needed, such as all kinds of documents, pens and paper.
- Reduce the (6) _____ noise.
- Ask people to repeat or (7) _____ things, spell words and speak slowly.
- Check everything to make sure it's all clear.
- Send a fax or an email after the phone call to be sure that there are no (8) _____.

*Useful expressions:*

- Spelling: I'm afraid I didn't (9) _____ your name. Could you spell it?
- Repeating: I'm sorry. I didn't catch that. Could you say that again?
- Repeating: I'm sorry. Could you repeat it?
- Speaking slowly: Could you speak a (10) _____ _____ _____?
- Checking: I will just check if I've understood everything. The venue is the Hilton Hotel. Is that correct?
- Checking: In other words, you can't (11) _____ the price at all. Is that right?
- Checking: Have I made myself understood?
- Explaining: I'm sorry. What do you mean by that? Could you explain it?
- Email confirmation: Could you send an email to (12) _____ our talk?

# Part 2  Business Speaking

## A Pair work

In *Table One* there are examples of fractions (分数), decimals (小数), percentages, phone numbers, reference numbers, sums of money, prices, measurements, and exchange rates. Read the figures and symbols in *Table One* and practice saying the figures and symbols in *Table Two* to your partner.

*Table One*

| / (slash/stroke) | 8% (eight percent) | $1.05 (one point zero 5 dollars) |
|---|---|---|
| 20 m × 14 m (twenty meters by fourteen meters) | 1.25% (one and a quarter percent) | 1.06% (one point zero six percent) |
| November 12 (Am: November twelfth; Br: The twelfth of November) | $1.54 – £ (one point five four dollars to the pound) | SW/567GF (SW Slash 567GF) |

CBE | 129

A: What's your turnover?
B: Our turnover is one million five hundred and seventy six thousand six hundred and forty five dollars.

*Table Two*

| Turnover | $ 1,576,645 |
| --- | --- |
| Interest rate | $5^{1/2}$ % |
| Measurements | 3 m × 5 m |
| Account number | SW/567GF |
| Delivery date | 5 November |
| Discount | 11.05% |
| Exchange rate | $ 1.56 – £ |

## B Role play

**Task One:** Jim Prior and Sally Ortega are discussing prices and discounts on the phone. You are Jim Prior. Your partner is Sally Ortega. Role-play a conversation according to the following situations. After the practice, change roles.

Jim Prior

Florida Marine will order 3,000 kg of Prime glass per month for a year at a base price of $ 190 per 100 kg.

Telephone Sally Ortega with your order. You want the following conditions:

　　Discount: 6.5%

　　If you order more than 3,000 kg a month, extra discount of 3%;

　　Delivery in three days.

Note down what you agree:

　　Base price: $ 190 per 100 kg;

　　Discount: _____ %;

　　If you order more than 3,000 kg a month, extra discount of _____ %;

　　Delivery in _____ .

Unit 10

|  Sally Ortega | Jim Prior will telephone you.<br>Find out what Jim Prior's offer is.<br>Discuss prices and conditions. You want the following conditions:<br>　　Discount: _____ ;<br>　　If they order more than 3,000 kg a month, extra discount of _____ ;<br>　　Delivery in _____ days.<br>Note down what you agree:<br>　　Base price: $ 190 per 100 kg;<br>　　Discount: _____ %;<br>　　If you order more than 3,000 kg a month, extra discount of _____ %;<br>　　Delivery in _____ . |

*Task Two:* You are each going to make a short presentation according to the following information. Try to use the expressions provided.

*Information for you:*

**What is important when negotiating a deal?**
- Getting the lowest possible price
- Achieving a "win-win" situation
- Being able to cancel the deal at any time

Useful expressions:
- I think that (X) is very important because...
- I don't think (Y) is important because...
- It's really useful/important to have...

*Information for your partner:*

**What is important when deciding how to transport goods?**
Reliability and safety
Speed of delivery
Costs

Useful expressions:
I think that (X) is very important because...
I don't think (Y) is important because...
It's really useful/important to have...

# Part 3 　 Listening Practice

## A Listening focus

### Guessing Meanings While Listening

*Task One:* Listen to the following dialogues and choose the best answer to each question you hear.

(1) W: Have you ever tried kayaking? It is so thrilling to hit the rapids.
　　M: Yes. It's been my favorite water sport since I was eleven.
　　Q: What is kayaking?
　　A. A famous book.
　　B. A pop song.
　　C. A mountain.
　　D. A kind of sport.

(2) M: The tickets for the concert sold off just before I got there. I would have got one if I hadn't stopped for a drink on the way.
　　W: Well, my roommate decided to pull out of going. You can have hers for what it cost her.
　　Q: What does "*to pull out of going*" mean?
　　A. To pull a ticket out.
　　B. To buy a ticket.
　　C. To move out of her apartment.
　　D. Not to go to the concert.

(3) M: Uh, could I borrow a few dollars until payday? I'm a little strapped for cash.
　　W: OK. But your friend Ron said you borrowed money from him last week. How are things going anyway?
　　Q: What does the man mean?
　　A. He has no money available.
　　B. He has nothing to eat.
　　C. He wants to go camping.
　　D. He is not used to taking cash with him.

(4) W: Wow, I was thrilled to receive such a thoughtful gift from Karen.
　　M: Yeah, she really has a heart of gold.
　　Q: What does the man mean?
　　A. Her heart is made of gold.
　　B. She is very kind to others.
　　C. The color of her heart is golden.

132 ┃ Unit 10　*What would you like to order*

D. She is very attractive.
(5) W: How was your driving test yesterday?
   M: Oh, well, the examiner was quite strict about traffic rules. I guess I didn't measure up.
   Q: What does "*to measure up*" mean?
   A. To measure the distance.
   B. To pass.
   C. To count how many rules he had asked me.
   D. To pay enough attention to him.

> *Task Two:* Listen carefully and match the words and phrases in Column A with their respective meanings in Column B.

| A | B |
| --- | --- |
| flick | someone who spends a lot of time sitting and watching television |
| awesome | go to sleep |
| airhead | someone who behaves in a stupid way |
| couch potato | movie |
| hit the sack | wonderful or great |

## B Dictation

> *Task One:* Listen to the short passage twice and fill in the blanks with the missing words or sentences.

- If using a touch-tone, press random numbers while ordering. Ask the person taking (1) _____ to stop doing that.
- Make up a charge-card name. Ask if they accept it.
- Give them your address, exclaim "Oh, just surprise me!" and (2) _____ .
- Do not spell them out; (3) _____ the toppings you want.
- (4) _____
- Ask what the order taker is wearing.
- Say hello, act stunned for five seconds, then behave as if they called you.
- Tell the (5) _____ you're depressed. Get him/her to (6) _____ .
- Change your accent every three seconds.
- (7) _____ , say "OK. That'll be $10.99; please pull up to the first window."
- Ask if you get to keep the (8) _____ . When they say yes, heave a sigh of relief.

*Task Two:* You're going to hear five sentences. Repeat each sentence you hear. Then listen again and write down each sentence. Check your answer when you listen for the third time.

(1) Owing to heavy commitments, we cannot accept fresh orders.
(2) For most of the articles in the catalogue, we have a good supply.
(3) We are interested in discussing arts and crafts business with you.
(4) We give a five percent discount for orders of a hundred or more.
(5) I'm your server today. May I bring you something to begin with?

## ⒸConversations

**Conversation 1**

*Task One:* Listen to the conversation and choose the best answer to each question.

(1) When does the conversation take place?
    A. In the morning.      B. In the afternoon.
    C. At noon.      D. In the evening.
(2) Where does the conversation take place?
    A. In the office.    B. In a factory.    C. At a trade fair.    D. At home.
(3) Who will open a letter of credit?
    A. The buyer.    B. The seller.    C. The banker.    D. The manager.
(4) When will the buyer pay for the mobile phones?
    A. When they get the mobile phones.
    B. As soon as the mobile phones are delivered.
    C. Before the delivery.
    D. After they open the letter of credit.
(5) What will they do at the end of the conversation?
    A. Sign a contract.
    B. Hold a dinner party to celebrate it.
    C. Discuss other terms.
    D. Fill out the purchase order.

*Task Two:* Listen to the conversation again and fill in the table with what you hear.

```
Name of the products: _____
Quantities: _____
Discount: _____
Delivery time: _____
Mode of payment: _____
```

# Unit 10

**Conversation 2**

*Task One:* Listen to the conversation and choose the best choice to complete each statement.

(1) The conversation happens { in the office. / on the phone.

(2) The customer learns about the item from { a catalog. / window shopping.

(3) Shipping charges { will be paid when the customer gets the sheets. / are included in the price.

(4) Kelly will pay by { Master card. / Visa.

(5) Doris will get { Kelly's e-mail address / Kelly's address } in a moment.

*Task Two:* Listen to the conversation again and fill in the table with what you hear.

The item Kelly wants to order

| Satin Sheets | |
|---|---|
| Where in the catalog | _____ |
| Size | Full set of sheets in _____ |
| Color | _____ |
| Production No. | _____ |
| Total cost | _____ |

## D Passage

*Task One:* Listen to the passage once and tick (√) the statements you hear indicating how to be a good listener.

(1) To make up your face.  ( )
(2) To act like a good listener.  ( )
(3) To use as many gestures as possible.  ( )
(4) Besides ears, other organs on your face should also be applied when listening.  ( )
(5) To look at the speaker while you are listening.  ( )
(6) To use verbs to show your reaction.  ( )
(7) To pay attention to the speaker.  ( )
(8) To show your emotion when you are listening.  ( )

**Task Two:** Listen to the passage again and fill in the chart with the information you have learned.

| Receptive equipment on a face | |
|---|---|
| Non-verbal signals | Eye-contact; |

# Part 4 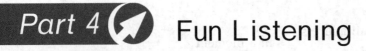 Fun Listening

**Task One:** Listen to the tongue twister and try to follow it.

I wish to wish the wish you wish to wish, but if you wish the wish the witch wishes, I won't wish the wish you wish to wish.

**Task Two:** Listen and read the poem after the tape.

### Poem About Economist
Kenneth E. Boulding

If you do some acrobatics
with a little mathematics
it will take you far along.
If your idea's not defensible
don't make it comprehensible
or folks will find you out,
and your work will draw attention
if you only fail to mention
what the whole thing is about.

You must talk of GNP
and of elasticity
of rates of substitution
and undeterminate solution
and oligonopopsony.

# Unit 11 We can make delivery in June

## Unit Goals

- Talking about delivery time
- Talking about shipment
- Understanding gifting culture and advice on gift giving
- Listening for key words
- Discussing delivery time

## Part 1  Practical Listening & Speaking

### A  Word study

Work with your partner to fill in the blanks using the words on the left. Listen and check your answers, and then follow the recording.

| make delivery |
| liner space |
| balance |
| Shipment |
| give top priority to |
| close the transaction |
| consult with |
| go through the terms |
| unloaded |

(1) Can we _____ _____ _____ _____ now?

(2) We promise to _____ _____ _____ _____ your order.

(3) I'm afraid I can't give you _____ _____ _____. I'll have to report to my boss first.

(4) I'm afraid it would be difficult for us to _____ _____ _____.

(5) Of course, we prefer _____ _____ _____. Could you arrange one for us?

(6) I can't make the decision now. I have to _____ _____ my manager.

(7) The _____ _____ is very difficult to book at the moment.

(8) Could you _____ _____ by the end of July? We are in urgent need of the goods.

(9) If you'd like us to arrange shipment, I'm afraid you'll have to pay _____ _____.

137

| |
|---|
| Transshipment |
| extra charges |
| a direct vessel |
| a firm reply |
| forwarding agent |

(10) I will contact our _____ _____ right away.
(11) We'll deliver the first lot in May and the _____ in June.
(12) Which port would you like your goods to be _____ at?
(13) _____ is a load of goods sent by sea, road, or air, or the act of sending them.
(14) _____ means goods have to be transshipped at another port before they reach the destination port.

## B Functional listening

*Task One (Talking about delivery time):* Listen to the recording and fill in the blanks.

Ben: When can you make delivery?
Lily: You can have the first five thousand units by April 30$^{th}$.
Ben: We need the whole ten thousand by April 30$^{th}$.
Lily: Well, (1) _____. You see we have a lot of orders to handle at present, and we've promised to give top priority to your order.
Ben: OK. What about the balance of the order? What's the earliest time you can deliver?
Lily: We can (2) _____ in three shipments over the following three months.
Ben: That'll be too late for us. We need them by May 31$^{st}$.
Lily: I'm afraid it'll be very difficult because the manufacturer has received a lot of orders this year. The workers are actually working (3) _____.
Ben: If we can't have all the goods by May 31$^{st}$, I'm afraid it would be difficult to close the transaction.
Lily: Well, I'm afraid you are really asking us for something that's very difficult. I'll (4) _____ and we'll find out if any special arrangements might be made for you.
Ben: Thanks. If you can promise delivery by May 31$^{st}$, then we may be able to talk about a further order.
Lily: If you can (5) _____, I think we could accept your terms.
Ben: Let's go through the terms: first five thousand units by

April 30<sup>th</sup> and the other five thousand units by May 31<sup>st</sup>.

Lily: Exactly. And you promise to place another order. Could we confirm this in writing?

Ben: Sure.

> Task Two (Talking about shipment): Listen to the conversation and complete the following notes using one or two words from the recording.

The woman says the liner space for Britain by the end of June has been _____ _____.

The man agrees to have the goods transshipped in _____ _____.

The man knows KAC Shipping Agent has a liner _____ _____ Britain around mid-June.

The woman promises to give the man a reply _____ _____.

## ⓒ Language check

> Work with your partner to complete the following conversations. Then listen and check your answers.

### Task One: Talking about delivery time

*Asking for the delivery date*

F: Could you tell me when you can make delivery?
M: We can deliver the goods by June 30<sup>th</sup>.

*Asking for the earliest delivery date*

F: I'm afraid that's too late. What is the soonest/earliest you can (1) _____?
M: Well, we can deliver the goods by June 20<sup>th</sup> at the earliest.

*Giving a new delivery date*

F: I'm afraid it's still too late. As you know, we need the goods badly. Can you make delivery before June 1<sup>st</sup>?
M: I'm afraid we can't. We have a lot of orders to fill at present, but we promise to give (2) _____ _____ to your order.

*Asking to advance delivery*

F: At least could you advance the shipment by 10 days? That's June 10<sup>th</sup>.

M: We'll try our best, but we can't give you a (3) _____ reply now.

*Giving the delivery deadline*

F: I'm afraid we really need the goods by June 10th at the (4) _____, or we'll have to look elsewhere.

M: OK. We'll see what we can do.

*Offering conditionally*

F: If you can promise delivery (5) _____ June 10th, then we may be able to talk about a further order.

M: If you can promise another order, I think we could (6) _____ your terms.

*Clarifying the position*

F: Let's go (7) _____ the terms: delivery by June 10th. Is that right?

M: Yes, exactly.

**Task Two: Talking about shipment**

*Talking about liner space*

F: Can you book shipping (1) _____ for us?

M: Yes, of course. But as far as I know, the liner space for Britain up to the end of June has been booked (2) _____.

*Talking about transshipment*

F: Oh, that's a pity. Is there any (3) _____ of transshipment?

M: Yes, you can have the goods transshipped in Hong Kong.

*Promising to contact the forwarding agent*

F: Could you make all the arrangements for us?

M: Yes, of course. I'll ask the shipping department to get in (4) _____ with our forwarding agent right away.

*Talking about the unloading port*

F: Thanks a lot.

M: Which port would you like the goods to be unloaded (5) _____?

F: We prefer London as the unloading port.

# D Controlled practice

You are a buyer. Your partner is a seller. Work together to make a dialogue based on the following flow chart. Listen to the recording of a model answer, and then follow it.

| YOU |
| --- |
| Ask for the earliest delivery time. |
| Say it's too late. Ask him/her to deliver in May. |
| Say you would look elsewhere if the goods can't be delivered in May. |
| Say you will place further orders if the goods can be delivered in May. |
| Ask to clarify the position. |

| YOUR PARTNER |
| --- |
| Say "by the end of June". |
| Say it's difficult. |
| Say you need to talk to your boss. |
| Say you can accept the terms. |
| Agree. |

# E Business culture

Work with your partner to answer the following questions. Then listen to the recording and fill in the blanks.

(1) When you attend a dinner party, do you often bring a gift to the host or hostess? What do you usually bring?
(2) What kinds of gifts are acceptable and unacceptable in the Chinese culture?
(3) What kinds of gifts are acceptable in the Western culture?

### Understanding Gifting Culture

Gifting is quite popular in the business world. A businessperson will usually bring a gift to the host/hostess when attending a dinner party. Doing this can undoubtedly (1) _____ business relationships. However, differences in cultures and (2) _____ should be taken into account when gifting takes place in a global (3) _____, and different cultures have different gifting habits. When gifting is not (4) _____ acceptable, it can ruin rather than improve business relations. Here are a few tips for you.

In China, give your gift with both hands. Don't give clocks, knives, (5) _____ or white, blue or black items. If someone gives you a gift, open it later in (6) _____. In America, if you receive a gift, open it right away while the other person is (7) _____. In the UK it's not customary to give gifts, but if you go to someone's home, take a bottle of wine or some (8) _____.

In Germany, if you're invited to someone's house, buy flowers for the (9) _____. Remove the wrapping before handing them to her. In Korea it is good (10) _____ to refuse a gift at first — people have to be (11) _____ to accept one. In Japan if you receive a gift, take it with both hands and open it later in private. If you give a gift (such as something from your country), it must be (12) _____ beautifully.

Generally, the perfect gift is something small and (13) _____ instead of something large and expensive. Maybe some (14) _____ food or drink from your country (e.g. Belgian chocolates or French wine), or a nicely wrapped product from your country (e.g. a crystal glass, china) will make a good gift for people from any culture. Best of all, give something you know the other person will really appreciate (e.g. a new DVD if she/he loves movies).

# Part 2  Business Speaking

## A Pair work

*Task One:* Read the conversation below. Work with your partner to put it into correct order, and then practice it.

(1) When can you make delivery?

(2) What's the earliest you can deliver?

(3) Can you advance shipment by one month?

(4) Can you advance the shipment date to July 10$^{th}$?

(5) Could you possibly make your delivery date not later than July 15$^{th}$?

A. We'll try our best, but we have to consult with our manufacturers. Is that OK if I give you a reply tomorrow?

B. I'm afraid July 10$^{th}$ is not possible. The goods are in short supply. We have no supply available for export.

C. We can make delivery in July.

D. We can deliver the goods by July 20$^{th}$ at the earliest. I'm afraid that's the best we can do.

E. I'm afraid one month is impossible.

Unit 11  *We can make delivery in June*

**Task Two:** Read the conversation below. Work with your partner to put it into correct order, and then practice it.

(1) Do you allow partial shipment?

(2) We can deliver 20% by the end of this month. The balance will have to be delivered over the next two months.

(3) Would you consider transshipment if there is no shipping space on direct vessels?

(4) Which port would you like the goods to be unloaded at?

(5) How about making Liverpool the unloading port? There are more sailings to Liverpool.

A. I'm afraid that's not good, as transshipment adds to the costs as well as the risk of damage.

B. We prefer London as the unloading port.

C. I'm afraid that's not possible. Liverpool is too far away from us.

D. That sounds fine.

E. Yes, we can consider that. How do you do that?

## B Role play

**Task One:** Your partner is a new employee, who knows little about international trade. Look at the pictures below and explain direct shipment and transshipment to him/her. After the practice, change roles.

A: What's transshipment?

B: Transshipment means that the goods are transshipped at a third port before they reach the unloading port.

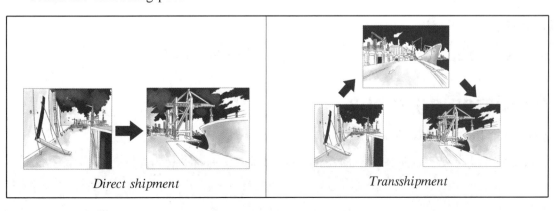

*Direct shipment*  *Transshipment*

**Task Two:** You and your partner are working in a company based in Shanghai. Your company is purchasing a batch of up-market garments (服装) from a company in Hong Kong. Discuss with your partner what is the best form of transportation of the garments.

A: What is the best form of transportation of the garments?
B: I think we should use air freight (空运) because it's the fastest.

*By sea*     *By air*     *By land*

**Task Three:** You are a seller. Your partner is a buyer. He/she asks you to advance shipment. You can't promise that because of the reasons which are listed in the table below. Practice the conversation. Change roles when it's finished.

A: Could you make delivery by July 5$^{th}$?
B: I'm afraid we can't. We are running short of stock. The goods are in high demand.

| We are running short of stock. The goods are in high demand. | The goods are in short supply. |
| --- | --- |
| There is no stock at the moment. The production was behind schedule. | The product hasn't gone into full production. |
| The supply can't satisfy the demand. | We have received a lot of orders. |
| There is no shipping space. | The vessel does not call at your port. |

# Part 3  Listening Practice

## Ⓐ Listening focus

### Listening for Key Words

**Task One:** Listen to a passage twice and complete the following statements about the features of a future car.

(1) There are _____ instead of 4 wheels on a car.
(2) The car is equipped with _____ .
(3) For the seats arrangement, _____ .
(4) _____ will automatically control the car.
(5) It is less likely for cars _____ .

*Task Two:* Listen to a conversation carefully and write down what a Coke addict is like.

A Coke addict $\begin{cases} \text{drinks 3 to 4 Cokes every day.} \\ \text{gets shaky and feels tense if he doesn't drink a Coke.} \end{cases}$

## B Dictation

*Task One:* Listen to the short passage twice and fill in the blanks with the missing words or sentences.

In a broad sense, logistics is the flow of goods, energy and information in a supply chain.

In an industrial (1) _____ , logistics means the art and science of obtaining, producing, and (2) _____ materials and products from a manufacturer to a customer in the most timely and cost-efficient manner possible.

Let's take McDonald's chain store as an example. (3) _____ ____ . It seems the logistical flow starts from the chicken farms. The chickens are caught in the farm at eleven p.m. under blue light, a light in which chickens cannot see. (4) _____ , where they are killed, dressed and frozen. Then they are taken to warehouses to be stored up for (5) _____ use.

When the McDonald's chain stores send out information on the (6) _____ of chicken needed, the transport center will design the (7) _____ route for the truck to go and the right quantity to carry for the truck, (8) _____ .

*Task Two:* You're going to hear five sentences. Repeat each sentence you hear. Then listen again and write down each sentence. Check your answer when you listen for the third time.

(1) _____
(2) _____
(3) _____
(4) _____
(5) _____

## C Conversations

**Conversation 1**

*Task One:* Listen to the conversation and fill in the chart with what you hear.

| Name of the commodity | |
|---|---|
| Selling season | |
| Delivery date | |

*Task Two:* Listen to the conversation again and answer the following questions.

(1) What are they discussing?

(2) Why can't the commodity be delivered earlier?

(3) What solution do they come to?

**Conversation 2**

*Task One:* Listen to the conversation and choose the best answer to each question.

(1) Why couldn't the seller effect the shipment earlier?
   A. There are fewer ships.
   B. The manufacturers are busy.
   C. There is a great demand for shipping space.
   D. The time for preparing shipment is not enough.

(2) Why is Mr. Smith worried about the transshipment?
   A. It will increase the expenses, risks of damage and may delay arrival.
   B. It will affect the selling season.
   C. It will spoil their fame.
   D. It will result in losing the goods.

(3) What is most important according to Mr. Smith?
   A. Good quality.　　　　　　B. Competitive price.
   C. Prompt shipment.　　　　D. Profit.

(4) Where will the goods be transshipped?
   A. London.　　B. New York.　　C. Paris.　　D. Liverpool.

(5) When will the goods be effected?

A. In a month.  B. Before the end of January.
C. In less than a month.  D. Later than January

*Task Two:* Listen to the conversation again and compare direct shipment and transshipment.

| Direct shipment | Transshipment |
| --- | --- |
| • _____<br>• _____<br>• _____ | • _____<br>• _____<br>• _____ |

# D Passage

*Task One:* Listen to the passage and decide whether the following statements are true (T) or false (F).

(1) If you know the host very well, you can bring a more expensive gift. (   )
(2) The bride will have "registered" at local department stores, so that she can buy something cheaper there. (   )
(3) When you leave to return to your home country, buy something made in the local country as a gift for your friends. (   )
(4) A book or something that reflects your culture can remind your friends of you when you go back to your home country. (   )
(5) You should not give anything too personal to your business acquaintance. (   )
(6) Clothing, especially a scarf, is the best for a business acquaintance. (   )

*Task Two:* Listen to the passage again and complete the table with what you hear.

| Occasions | Gift you can buy | Advantages |
| --- | --- | --- |
| Wedding | An item _____ _____ | The couple won't receive duplicate gifts. |
| A baby shower | An appropriate gift for _____ _____ | / |
| You go back to your home country | _____ _____ | It can remind of _____ _____ |
| At the office | Something appropriate _____ _____ | / |

# Part 4  Fun Listening

***Task One:*** Listen to the one-liners(俏皮话) and enjoy them.

A bad day fishing is better than a good day at work.
A bird in the bush usually has a friend in there with him.
A bird in the hand is dead.
A boss with no humor is like a job that is no fun.
A committee is a group that keeps minutes and loses hours.
A conclusion is the place where you got tired of thinking.
A conservative is a man with two perfectly good legs who has never learned to walk.
A consultant is an ordinary person a long way from home.
A couple of months in the lab can often save a couple of hours in the library.
A day without sunshine is like night.
A geophysicist is not drunk as long as he can hang onto a single blade of grass and not fall off the face of the earth.

# Unit 12 What about packing and insurance

## Unit Goals

- ◇ Talking about packing
- ◇ Talking about insurance
- ◇ Understanding the Chinese offer-decline culture
- ◇ Listening for specific details
- ◇ Understanding people talking about business insurance

# Part 1 Practical Listening & Speaking

## A Word study

Work with your partner to fill in the blanks using the words on the left. Listen and check your answers, and then follow the recording.

| Packaging |
| wrap |
| Packing |
| reinforce the cartons |
| strap |
| waterproof |
| withstand rough handling |
| covers |
| insure |
| Insurance premium |

(1) The extra fee is _____ _____ _____ _____.

(2) We will ask our workers to _____ _____ _____.

(3) The box is very strong. It can _____ _____ _____.

(4) _____ means that things are put into cases or boxes so that they can be sent or taken somewhere.

(5) _____ is the way in which something, such as products, is presented to the public.

(6) _____ _____ is the value to be insured.

(7) _____ _____ is the money that you pay regularly to an insurance company.

(8) _____ _____ is the amount of money on the invoice.

(9) If you _____ something, you put paper or cloth over it to cover it.

(10) When you _____ something, you fasten it using a narrow band of strong material.

149

| |
|---|
| for the buyer's account |
| Insurance value |
| Coverage |
| Invoice value |

(11) If your insurance _____ you, it promises to pay you money if you have an accident.

(12) If something is _____, water doesn't enter it.

(13) If you _____ something, you provide insurance for it.

(14) _____ is extent of protection afforded by an insurance policy.

## B Functional listening

*Task One (Talking about packing)*: Listen to the recording and fill in the blanks.

Dirk: First, about the packaging, how would you package the silk dresses?

Rita: We usually wrap each (1) _____ _____ and then put it in a beautifully-designed small box.

Dirk: Good. Could I have a look at the sample packaging?

Rita: Yes, of course. Here you are.

Dirk: Thanks. (2) _____. Then, what about the packing?

Rita: We pack 40 silk dresses into one carton.

Dirk: Carton? I'm afraid they are not strong enough for sea transportation.

Rita: You don't (3) _____. We'll reinforce the cartons with strong straps.

Dirk: Are they waterproof?

Rita: Yes. Each carton is (4) _____ _____ so that water can't get into it. Besides, we'll put a "Keep Dry" sign on the outside.

Dirk: Can they withstand rough handling?

Rita: Yes, I think so. (5) _____.

Dirk: OK. Since you are so confident about your packing, I accept cartons. But I do hope the goods will be fine when I receive them.

Rita: I'm sure they will be fine. Please trust me.

**Task Two (Talking about insurance):** Listen to the conversation and complete the following notes using one or two words from the recording.

(1) The woman's company will _____ WPA for the man's goods.
(2) Rainwater Damage risk is a _____ _____. The insurance value is 110% of the _____ value.
(3) The man has no more _____ about the insurance.

## ⓒ Language check

Work with your partner to complete the following conversations. Then listen and check your answers.

*Task One: Talking about packaging*

F: How would you package the goods?
M: We (1) _____ each of them in a wooden box.
F: Can you design the box according (2) _____ our instructions?
M: Yes, we can do that.

*Task Two: Talking about packing*

*Packing*

F: What about the packing?
M: We pack 20 dozen silk dresses (1) _____ one carton.

*Being seaworthy*

F: Are they seaworthy?
M: Yes. They are (2) _____ enough for sea transportation.

*Being waterproof*

F: Are they (3) _____?
M: Yes. Each carton is lined with plastic sheets so that water can't come into it.

*Withstanding rough handling*

F: Can they withstand (4) _____ handling?
M: Yes, I think so. They are very strong.

*Wooden cases*

F: Can you pack them in wooden cases?

M: Yes, we can. But wooden cases are heavy and more expensive. We'd better (5) _____ them in cartons of 5kg each instead of wooden cases of 20 kg.

*Markings*

F: What about markings? Can you (6) _____ the packages according to our instructions?

M: Yes, of course.

### Task Three: Talking about insurance

*Asking about coverage*

F: What coverage can you (1) _____ for the goods?

M: We cover All Risks for them.

F: Can you cover War Risk?

M: No, I'm afraid we don't (2) _____ the goods against War Risk.

*Asking about insurance value*

F: What about insurance (3) _____?

M: We usually insure the goods for 110% of the invoice value.

*Talking about insurance premium*

F: I'd like to have the goods insured (4) _____ 130% of the invoice value. Could you do that for me?

M: Yes, but I have (5) _____ out that we usually insure the goods for 110% of the invoice value. If you'd like 130%, the extra premium will be (6) _____ the buyer's account.

*Asking about the insurance company*

F: Which company do you insure the goods with?

M: We insure the goods (7) _____ the People's Insurance Company of China.

## D Controlled practice

You are a buyer. Your partner is a seller. Work together to make a dialogue based on the following flow chart. Listen to the recording of a model answer, and then follow it.

| YOU | YOUR PARTNER |
|---|---|
| Ask about the packaging. | Wrap each item in golden paper and put it in a plastic bag. |
| Ask about the packing. | Pack 20 bags into a cardboard box. |
| Ask if it's seaworthy. | It's seaworthy. It's reinforced with strong straps. |
| Ask if it's waterproof. | It's waterproof. It's wrapped in a strong plastic bag. |
| Ask if it can withstand rough handling. | It can withstand rough handling. |
| Ask about the coverage. | Cover All Risks for the goods. |
| Ask about the insurance value. | Insure the goods for 110% of the invoice value. |

## E Business culture

Work with your partner to answer the following questions. Then listen to the recording and fill in the blanks.

(1) When a Chinese person is offered something, for example, a drink, he or she usually declines it one or two times before accepting it. Do you think this is true?
(2) When a Westerner is offered something, for example, a drink, he or she usually accepts it directly if it's really needed. Do you think this is true?

*Offer-Decline* 3 *Times*: *Chinese Standing on Ceremony*

When I was a student in college, my classmates and I once visited our American teacher. It was a (1) _____ hot summer day. The twenty people including me made great efforts climbing the 150 steps to his hilltop apartment. Sweaty and gasping for (2) _____, we sprawled (平躺) on sofas, chairs and the floor.

"Would you like some tea?" our teacher asked. "Oh, no!" came the chorus from us. "We don't want to (3) _____ you!" "Are you sure?" he asked again. "No, too much trouble," we repeated hesitantly this time, for we were actually (4) _____ to death.

As he had stayed in China for a while, and learned a little bit of Chinese (5) _____, his common sense and our facial (6) _____ told him that we were desperate for something to drink, and we were just (7) _____ on ceremony. He offered a third time. "Are you sure you don't want tea? Raise your hands if you do." Then hands (8) _____ _____ everywhere. Some even raised two hands, as if they were being robbed. "Help yourself!" he said. We unceremoniously (随便地) raced for the teapot.

The above case is a perfect indication of the (9) _____ in etiquette between Chinese and English people. Chinese will behave courteously(礼貌地) by declining several times(Ke Qi) before accepting an offer or a (10) _____ from others. This is considered a polite way, which also makes the person who offers (11) _____. On the contrary, a Chinese who takes an offer for granted without the decline ritual(礼节) is usually (12) _____ as greedy and ignorant of basic Chinese etiquette.

However, English people are (13) _____. When they want what is offered, they will say "yes". When they don't, they will say "no". In their eyes, Chinese courtesy is (14) _____ and sometimes annoying, which may make them confused or cause misunderstanding. An understanding of this difference between the two cultures, therefore, is important for smooth communication.

# Part 2  Business Speaking

## A Pair work

*Task One:* There is a preposition missing from each of the following twelve sentences about packing and insurance. Work with your partner to fill in the blanks using the prepositions in the table below. Some of them may be used more than once. Then take turns to practice saying the sentences.

| in | into |
|---|---|
| about | for |
| against | to |
| with | |

(1) We usually wrap each item _____ a plastic bag and then put it _____ a beautifully designed small box.
(2) We pack 40 silk dresses _____ one carton.
(3) We'll reinforce the cartons _____ strong straps.
(4) Each carton is lined _____ plastic sheets so that water can't get into it.
(5) We can design the box according _____ your instructions.
(6) Since you are so confident _____ your packing, I accept cartons.

（7）We provide a wide coverage _____ the goods.
（8）We think it's not necessary to cover War Risk _____ the goods.
（9）We usually insure the goods _____ 110% of the invoice value.
（10）The extra premium will be _____ the buyer's account.
（11）I'm afraid we don't insure the goods _____ Rainwater Damage.
（12）We insure the goods _____ the People's Insurance Company of China.

*Task Two:* Ask the following twelve questions. Your partner answers them using the twelve sentences from *Task One*. Ask the questions again. This time your partner should try to answer them without looking at the book. After the practice, change roles.

How would you package the goods?
How would you pack the goods?
Are they seaworthy?
Are they waterproof?
Can you design the box according to our instructions?
So can you accept cartons for the packing?

Could you tell me what coverage you can provide for the goods?
Can you cover War Risk for the goods?
What's the insurance value?
Who will pay the extra premium?
Do you insure the goods against Rainwater Damage?
Which company do you insure the goods with?

# B Role play

*Task One:* Your company produces all kinds of china products. Look at the following pictures about inner packing（内包装）materials. Work with your partner to discuss which kind of inner packing material you will choose for your product.

A: How should we package our product?
B: I think we should use the silk bag.

| | | |
|---|---|---|
| <br>Carton（小纸板箱） | <br>Plastic bag | <br>Glossy（有光泽的）paper bag |
| <br>Cloth bag | <br>Wooden box（木盒子） | <br>Silk bag |

***Task Two:*** Your company produces all kinds of china products. Look at the following pictures about outer packing（外包装）materials. Work with your partner to discuss which kind of outer packing material you will choose for your product.

A: How should we pack our product?
B: I think we should use the wooden case.

| | | |
|---|---|---|
| <br>Cardboard box（纸板箱） | <br>Gunny bag（麻布袋） | <br>Wooden case（木箱） |
| <br>Metal case（金属箱） | <br>Iron drum（铁桶） | <br>Crate（板条箱） |

# Part 3  Listening Practice

## A Listening focus

### Listening for details

*Task One:* You're going to hear three short conversations between two speakers. At the end of each conversation, a question will be asked about what has been said. Listen carefully and answer the following questions with what you hear.

**Conversation 1**

(1) What's the woman's size?

_____

(2) What color does the woman prefer?

_____


**Conversation 2**

(1) What isn't working in the room?

_____

(2) Which room will the customer move in?

_____


**Conversation 3**

(1) When is the reservation for?

_____

(2) How many people will come to dinner?

_____

*Task Two:* Listen to the passage about A Young Woman's Diet and choose the best answer to each question.

(1) What does she like to have on her toast?
    A. Egg.    B. Butter and jam.    C. Omelet.    D. Cheese.
(2) What's her typical lunch?
    A. Sandwich.                     B. Chicken.
    C. Cereal and milk.        D. Fruits.
(3) What kind of fruit does she like?
    A. Grapes.    B. Oranges.    C. Plums.    D. Tomatoes.
(4) When does she have her main meal of the day?

A. At noon.  B. In the evening.
C. In the morning.  D. At night.
(5) What does she like for her dinner?
A. Steak.  B. Hamburgers.
C. Chicken.  D. Anything that has meat in it.

## B Dictation

*Task One:* Listen to the short passage twice and fill in the blanks with the missing words or sentences.

Packaging refers to the (1) _____ unit of issue, essentially the first wrap, bag or carton that completes a unit for sale or (2) _____. It starts with one wrap but can be an eight-ounce bag or a multi-pack case, (3) _____ on the client's needs.

Packing refers to the consolidation of packages into a final (4) _____ configuration. This can be a small UPS final carton or a Club Store Pallet Display. In the export and defense world, it could even be a heavy duty box (5) _____ a 10,000 pound machine destined for the Philippines.

Our company does it all. We are contract packaging and packing specialists. (6) _____, over 300,000 square feet of separate manufacturing and food grade distribution.

We have several high-speed wrappers with long conveyor in-feeds and many automatic bar sealers for short run custom projects. (7) _____. So whether it's a complex DVD studio box set or a simple Club Store Value Pack, (8) _____ wraps per day.

*Task Two:* You're going to hear five sentences. Repeat each sentence you hear. Then listen again and write down each sentence. Check your answer when you listen for the third time.

(1) _____
(2) _____
(3) _____
(4) _____
(5) _____

## C Conversations

**Conversation 1**

*Task One:* Listen to the conversation and choose the best answer to each question.

(1) How many kinds of packing has Mr. Wilson mentioned?

A. Two. B. Three.
C. Four. D. Five.

(2) Which packing is the most advanced packing in the world market?
A. Shrunk packaging. B. Skin packing.
C. Hanging packing D. Neutral packing.

(3) Products are packed in boxes of _____ dozen each, _____ boxes to a wooden case.
A. 3... 18... B. 13... 18...
C. 3... 80... D. 30... 80...

(4) The total weight of the packed goods will be over _____ kilograms.
A. 200. B. 1,200.
C. 20,000. D. 2,000.

(5) The client will open the L/C after he returns to _____.
A. Denmark B. Germany
C. France D. Turkey

*Task Two:* Listen to the conversation again and fill in the missing information.

(1) Mr. Wilson leads his client to the ☐.

(2) There are ☐ kinds of packing such as shrunk packaging, skin packing and hanging packing, etc.

(3) The client doubts whether the wooden case is strong enough for ☐.

(4) The goods can be packed according to the customer's ☐.

(5) Mr. Wilson will make the shipment as soon as he receives the ☐.

## Conversation 2

*Task One:* Listen to the conversation and decide whether the following statements are true or not. Mark (√) for the correct ones and (×) for the wrong ones.

(1) Ms. Lee usually does business with her customer on CIF basis.    (  )
(2) Mr. Hooper will arrange the insurance for himself.    (  )
(3) If Mr. Hooper requires a higher amount, he has to bear the additional premium.
    (  )
(4) The company Ms. Lee works for has many agencies abroad.    (  )
(5) Finally, Mr. Hooper doesn't insure his goods.    (  )

*Task Two:* Listen again and complete the answers to the following questions.

(1) How much will the premium of insurance be?
   It relies on _____.
(2) What kind of insurance will Ms. Lee arrange for soft cloth?
   _____ coverage.
(3) What is the usual insurance amount?
   _____.
(4) Which company does Ms. Lee usually insure with?
   _____.
(5) If any damage occurs, what can Mr. Hooper do?
   He can _____ after the arrival of the goods.

## D Passage

*Task One:* Listen to the passage carefully and fill in the blanks with the missing information.

(1) Insurance is a precaution against a possible unwanted outcome in _____ and in _____.
(2) People use insurance to protect against the possibility of _____, usually _____.
(3) After people buy insurance, they transfer risks to someone else in exchange for a _____ or _____.
(4) People couldn't run _____ or drive cars, _____ homes or _____ anywhere without insurance.
(5) Insurance gives people the _____ and _____ people need to operate.

*Task Two:* Listen to the passage again and complete the table below.

| | |
|---|---|
| (1) Early insurance can be traced back to ... | the _____ times. |
| (2) Why did Chinese merchants disperse their shipments with several vessels? | To _____. |
| (3) Some insurance companies in the U.S.A. provided insurance back in ... | _____. |
| (4) There is insurance for many aspects of daily living, such as ... | Business, Auto, _____, _____, and Travel. |
| (5) Insurance has many categories including ... | _____, which branch off into a great number of _____. |

# Part 4 Fun Listening

*Task One:* Listen to the insurance joke and tell the funny part of it.

A lawyer and an engineer were fishing in the Caribbean. The lawyer said, "I'm here because my house burned down, and everything I owned was destroyed by the fire. The insurance company paid for everything."

"That's quite a coincidence," said the engineer. "I'm here because my house and all my belongings were destroyed by a flood, and my insurance company also paid for everything."

The lawyer thought for a moment, but was puzzled. Finally he asked the engineer, "How do you start a flood?"

*Task Two:* Listen to the insurance joke and tell why the last salesman says so.

Three insurance salesmen were sitting in a restaurant boasting about each company's service.

The first one said, "When one of our insureds died suddenly on Monday, we got the news that evening and were able to process the claim for the wife and had mailed a check on Wednesday evening."

The second one said, "When one of our insureds died without warning on Monday, we learned of it in 2 hours and were able to hand-deliver a check the same evening."

The last salesman said, "That's nothing. Our office is on the 20th floor of a tall building. One of our insureds who was washing a window on the 85th floor, slipped and fell. We handed him his check as he passed our floor."

# Unit 13 Shall we sign the contract

Unit Goals
- ◇ Signing a contract
- ◇ Learning tips for making a toast
- ◇ Understanding people talking about a contract
- ◇ Understanding what a contract is
- ◇ Listening for the main idea

## Part 1  Practical Listening & Speaking

### A Word study

Work with your partner to fill in the blanks using the words on the left. Listen and check your answers, and then follow the recording.

|  | |
|---|---|
| signing the contract | (1) _____ is a part of a written law or legal document covering a particular subject of the whole law or document. |
| drafted a sales contract | (2) I hope everything will go smoothly during the _____ _____ _____ _____. |
| Arbitration | (3) We need to make sure everything is all right before _____ _____ _____. |
| Clause | (4) Full-time employees _____ _____ _____ receive health insurance. |
| comply with | (5) I need to _____ _____ _____ before we sign it. |
| are entitled to | (6) I'd like to _____ _____ _____ at the airport. |
| terminate the contract | (7) If one party fails to obey the terms of the contract, the other party has the right to _____ _____ _____. |
| modify the contract | (8) _____ is the process of judging officially how an argument should be settled. |
| original | (9) We've _____ _____ _____ _____ according to our discussions. |

Unit 13

| execution of the contract |
|---|
| toast |
| treat |
| stuffed |
| see you off |
| board a plane |

(10) When you _____ _____ something, you do what you are supposed to do according to a law or agreement.

(11) When you _____ _____ _____, you get onto the plane.

(12) If something is _____, it's completely new and different from anything that anyone has thought of before.

(13) If you drink a _____ to others, you drink something in order to thank them and wish them good luck.

(14) I'd like to _____ you to dinner sometime next week.

(15) When you are _____, you can't eat any more.

## B Functional listening

*Task One (Signing a contract):* Listen to the recording and fill in the blanks.

Rose: We have drafted a sales contract based on the results of our talks. Could you have a look to see if there's any misunderstanding?

Jack: Sure. Thanks.

*(A few minutes later)*

Rose: Is everything all right?

Jack: I think (1) _____ except some minor points. One thing is about arbitration.

Rose: So what's wrong with it?

Jack: I think we agreed that (2) _____ in a third country, in Sweden. But in the contract, it says "China".

Rose: I'm sorry. That must've been a mistake. I'll correct it right away. Anything else?

Jack: I think we should (3) _____ the contract. That is "If one party fails to comply with the terms of the contract, the other party is entitled to terminate the contract".

Rose: (4) _____. Anything else?

Jack: No, that's all.

Rose: OK. Could you excuse me for a minute? I'll modify the contract and have it ready in a moment.

Jack: Yes, of course. Take your time.

(*A few minutes later*)

Rose: Here is the modified contract. (5) _____?

Jack: Yes, I've been looking forward to this moment.

Rose: After you. Please sign your name here, here and here.

Jack: Thank you.

Rose: Now each of us has (6) _____ the contract: one in Chinese and the other in English. You may keep these copies.

Jack: Thank you very much. I hope everything will go smoothly during the execution of the contract.

*Task Two (Toasting at a farewell dinner):* Listen to the conversation and complete the following notes using one or two words from the recording.

(1) The man has been looking forward to a real _____ _____.

(2) The man thinks the food is delicious. He loves _____ _____.

(3) They can enjoy the "color, flavor and _____" of the food at the same time.

(4) The man will leave _____.

(5) The woman _____ the man _____ at the airport.

(6) The woman wishes the man a _____ and _____ journey home.

## C Language check

Work with your partner to complete the following conversations. Then listen and check your answers.

### Task One: Signing a contract

*Asking to restate the terms*

F: Shall we repeat all the terms we have discussed?

M: Yes, of course.

F: Shall we go (1) _____ all the details to see if we agree on all of them?

M: OK.

*Asking the other party to check the contract*

F: We'll prepare a contract and have it (2) _____ to your hotel for you to go through.

M: Thank you.
F: We've prepared the (3) _____ according to what we have discussed. Please take a look at it before we sign it.
M: OK. Thanks.

*Asking the other party to modify the contract*

M: I think the shipment (4) _____ should be modified.
F: OK. How should we improve it?
M: I think we should (5) _____ one more point to it: shipment should be made by July 1st.
F: OK. I'll do it right away.

*Singing the contract and giving good wishes*

F: I'm glad that our (6) _____ has come to a successful conclusion. Shall we sign the contract?
M: Yes, I've been looking forward to this moment.
F: And I hope (7) _____ will go smoothly during the execution of the contract.
M: Yes, I'm sure it will.

**Task Two: Toasting at a farewell dinner**

*Inviting*

F: Today, we'd like to treat you (1) _____ dinner at a Chinese restaurant.
M: Thank you. I'd (2) _____ to.

*Helping yourself*

F: Please help yourself (3) _____ whatever you like.
M: Thanks, I will.

*Toasting*

F: Here's a toast to our successful cooperation. (4) _____.
M: Cheers.
F: Let's raise our glasses and drink to our close cooperation. Cheers.
M: Cheers.
F: I'd like to propose a (5) _____ to Mr. Jones! Bottoms up!
M: Thank you. Bottoms up!

Task Three: Seeing someone off at the airport

*Thanking*

F: I can't believe you're leaving tomorrow. I (1) _____ you could stay longer.

M: I wish I could. I've enjoyed being here. Thank you for making my (2) _____ so pleasant. I've really enjoyed working with you here.

F: I'm glad you (3) _____ your stay here. It was also a great pleasure to work with you.

*Bidding farewell*

M: And thank you so much for coming to see me (4) _____.

F: My pleasure. I wish you a safe and pleasant (5) _____ home.

M: Thanks a lot. Goodbye!

F: Bye-bye.

## D Controlled practice

You are a seller. Your partner is a buyer. Work together to make a dialogue based on the following flow chart. Listen to the recording of a model answer, and then follow it.

| YOU | YOUR PARTNER |
| --- | --- |
| Ask him/her to have a look at the contract. | Agree. |
| Ask if it's OK. | Say it seems fine except one minor point. |
| Ask what's wrong. | Say the insurance clause should be modified. |
| Ask how to modify it. | Say he/she should cover All Risks instead of WPA for the goods. |
| Agree to modify it. | Say "Thanks". |
| Ask him/her to sign the contract. | Agree. |
| Give good wishes. | Respond. |

## E Business culture

Work with your partner to answer the following questions. Then listen to the recording and fill in the blanks.

(1) Do you know why and when people make a toast?
(2) Do you know the toasting differences between Chinese and Western cultures? What are they?
(3) What are the appropriate expressions you can use when making a toast in English?

---

*Tips for Making a Toast*

Toasting can be traced back to ancient times. The ancient Greeks and Romans raised a glass to protect themselves from (1) _____ _____. Early Christians（基督教徒）toasted to keep Satan（撒旦）away. In the Middle Ages, when people poisoned enemies, toasting was a polite way of (2) _____ that the wine was safe to drink.

Toasting is an art. When you toast, you should do it gracefully, saying something beautiful with seeming (3) _____. To be sure you make an appropriate toast, here are some (4) _____ for you to make a good one.

Put some effort into it. If someone asks you to make a toast, it's your (5) _____ and you ought to do a little homework. Choose your words (6) _____ because people really are listening. A toast is a small speech. A (7) _____ toast should have an opening, a body, and a conclusion. The best toasts are original and heartfelt（真心真意的）.

Keep it short and (8) _____. People don't like standing there for too long while you are making a long speech. They are (9) _____ their glasses in the air. They want to drink wine. A well-planned toast should never last longer than 60 seconds. And never read your toast. If it's too long to remember, it's too long.

Make sure the toast is appropriate for the (10) _____. You need to be clear about the reason. Is it to be entertaining or meaningful? Is it for giving new year's wishes or bidding farewell? For example, a (11) _____ new year's toast looks backward and forward. The main thing is to express high hopes for the new year and happy (12) _____ of the past year.

Here are some good toasting examples for business and other purposes:

(1) To our pleasant cooperation! I'd like to suggest a toast. (2) To our cooperation and friendship! Cheers! (3) Let's raise our glasses and drink to our successful cooperation! (4) Let's drink to the growth and prosperity of your cooperation. Cheers! (5) I would like to propose a toast to Mr. Johnson. You have done so much to develop the relationship between our companies. Bottoms up!

(1) To your health! Cheers! (2) To your pleasant trip home! Cheers! (3) To our friendship! (4) Here's a toast to the future, a toast to the past! (5) Here's a toast to our friends, far and near. May the future be pleasant, the past a bright dream. (6) Here's to turkey when you're hungry, champagne when you're dry, a lover when you need one, and heaven when you die.

# Part 2  Business Speaking

## A Pair work

*Task One:* Read the conversation below. Work with your partner to put it into correct order, and then practice it.

(1) I believe you must have read the draft contract we sent you yesterday.

(2) Do you think there's anything that needs to be modified?

(3) What is it?

(4) OK. We'll add that condition. Is there anything else?

A. No, the rest is perfect. Thank you for your cooperation.

B. Regarding the delivery time, we wish to add "Delivery should be made no later than July 31$^{st}$".

C. Yes. Thank you.

D. Everything is all right except that one condition needs to be added.

*Task Two:* Work with your partner to match each expression in *Table One* with its meaning in *Table Two*. Then say the sentences in *Table One*, and your partner should try to respond with the similar sentences in *Table Two* without looking at the book. After the practice, change roles.

Table One

| |
|---|
| (1) What can I get you? |
| (2) That sounds nice. |
| (3) How's yours? |
| (4) Just a drop, thanks. |
| (5) It's an acquired taste. |
| (6) Nothing to start with, thanks. |
| (7) No, I'm all right, thanks. |
| (8) Please start. |
| (9) Where's the loo here? |
| (10) This one's on me. |
| (11) No, no, I insist. |

*Table Two*

| | |
|---|---|
| A. From your description, I think I'm going to like this dish. | |
| B. Can you tell me where the restroom is? | |
| C. No, thank you. I don't want any more. | |
| D. I'll have just a little more wine. Thank you. | |
| E. Please don't wait for me. | |
| F. You must let me pay for the dinner. | |
| G. What would you like to drink? | |
| H. It's unusual and you may not like it at first. | |
| I. I'd like to pay. | |
| J. What is your meal like? | |
| K. I don't want a starter. Thank you. | |

## B Role play

Read the statements about contracts in *Table Three*. Work with your partner to fill in the blanks using the words in *Table Two*. Ask the questions in *Table One* below, and your partner answers them. After the practice, change roles.

*Table One*

| |
|---|
| What's a contract? |
| What's a breach of contract? |
| What's the difference between arbitration and litigation(诉讼)? |
| How can a contract be terminated? |

*Table Two*

| | | |
|---|---|---|
| period | court | ways |
| clauses | court | case |
| agreement | parties | sections |

*Table Three*

A contract is an _____ reached between two parties. It is divided into _____, clauses, and conditions.
The contract provides for(规定) any problem between the two _____. The conditions of the contract are binding(有约束力的) on both parties. If one party does not abide by(comply

> with) the _____, this is called a breach (违反) of contract.
> In the _____ of a dispute (争议), many contracts provide for arbitration, but in some cases the dispute results in litigation. Most parties reach a compromise (妥协) without going to _____, and the dispute is settled out of _____.
> Some contracts are for a fixed _____, or term; also, there are _____ in which the parties can end or terminate the contract.

# Part 3  Listening Practice

## A Listening focus

**Listening for the main idea**

*Task One:* You are going to hear two speakers talking about different topics. Listen carefully and give a brief answer to each question below.

(1) What is the main information provided by the first speaker?
_____

(2) What is the second speaker mainly talking about?
_____

*Task Two:* Listen to a short passage and write down the main idea of it.
_____

## B Dictation

*Task One:* Listen to the short passage twice and fill in the blanks with the missing words or sentences.

A contract is often seen as the (1) _____, but in fact, a properly drawn contract can be your friend. It should be written clearly and (2) _____ to protect both parties. The reality is that well-written contracts serve to (3) _____ the work to be done, and perhaps not to be done. They outline who is responsible for certain (4) _____ and how to handle changed orders. They set a (5) _____ time frame. In addition, they can serve as a record to remind the parties involved about all the agreed-upon details. In short, (6) _____. It should be detailed in a factual way. It should reference all relevant documents. (7) _____ of approaching dispute resolution. And (8) _____. Executed in

Unit 13

this fashion, a good contract can be an ally for all involved.

> **Task Two:** You're going to hear five sentences. Repeat each sentence you hear. Then listen again and write down each sentence. Check your answer when you listen for the third time.

(1) _____.

(2) _____.

(3) _____.

(4) _____.

(5) _____.

## C Conversations

**Conversation 1**

> **Task One:** Listen to the conversation and correct the mistakes in the following sentences.

(1) Miss Simpson hasn't looked over the contract yet.
   [                                                                 ]
(2) According to the contract, only a part of employees can get a discount in the restaurant.
   [                                                                 ]
(3) Miss Simpson doesn't get any copy of the contract.
   [                                                                 ]
(4) The man has prepared the contract for Miss Simpson to sign beyond her understanding.
   [                                                                 ]
(5) Finally, Miss Carol Simpson refuses the job.
   [                                                                 ]

> **Task Two:** Listen to the conversation again and answer the following questions.

(1) How many hours will Carol Simpson work a week according to the contract?

_____

(2) How many days will Miss Simpson work a week, if she accepts the job?

_____

(3) What is the salary the job offers?

_____

(4) What benefits will Miss Simpson have under the contract?

_____

(5) Is Carol Simpson's membership different from paying club members?
_____

## Conversation 2

*Task One:* Listen to the conversation and choose the best answer to complete each of the following statements.

(1) The goods are _____.
　　A. color TV sets, 30 inches　　　B. color TV sets, 32 inches
　　C. color TV sets, 23 inches　　　D. color TV sets, 20 inches
(2) The unit price is _____.
　　A. US $ 300 per set CIF San Francisco
　　B. US $ 300 per set CIF Santiago
　　C. US $ 200 per set CIF San Francisco
　　D. US $ 200 per set CIF Santiago
(3) The shipment is to be made in 3 equal monthly installments of _____ from Feb. 2007.
　　A. 40,000 sets　　　B. 30,000 sets
　　C. 20,000 sets　　　D. 10,000 sets
(4) The outer packing is to be strengthened by _____.
　　A. jute rope　　　B. nylon straps
　　C. sisal rope　　　D. plastic straps
(5) The insurance covers _____.
　　A. AR and T.P.N.D.　　　B. All Risks and WPA
　　C. AR and FPA　　　D. All Risks and F.W.R.D.

*Task Two:* Listen to the conversation again and fill in the contract.

---

**Sales Contract**

**Commodity:** Color TV
**Quantity:** (1) _____
**Total price:** (2) US $ _____
**Payment:** (3) L/C payable against presentation of _____.
**Packing:**
Each TV set is to be wrapped in a (4) _____ fixed with plastic padding and put in a carton.
**Insurance:**
To be effected with PICC for (5) _____ against All Risks and T.P.N.D.

## D Passage

*Task One:* Listen to the passage and decide whether the following statements are true (T) or false (F).

(1) A contract is a legally binding, written agreement spelling out obligations to each party. (　　)
(2) A contract can also be written on a plain sheet of paper. (　　)
(3) Under no circumstances can a contract be changed. (　　)
(4) Deal with only reputable individuals or companies. (　　)
(5) When the term "guaranteed" is used alone, it means a lot. (　　)

*Task Two:* Listen to the passage again and fill in the missing information.

A contract is a written agreement signed by (1) _____ parties. Once it is in force it generally can't be (2) _____. So, before you sign a contract, be sure you really need, want and can afford the (3) _____ for which you are signing. Be sure you understand every word it contains. If you do not, get a lawyer to help you. It is also necessary to make sure you (4) _____ of the contract. If you have any doubts, do not sign. Be sure you understand exactly what the seller is to do for you. Be sure the terms and conditions are spelled out clearly. Never let yourself (5) _____. Above all, make sure to deal only with reputable businesses.

# Part 4　Fun Listening

*Task One:* Listen to the story "New CEO" and then answer the question "What is the message in each envelope?"

Envelope 1

Envelope 2

Envelope 3

# Unit 14 When can you make the payment

## Unit Goals
◇ Chasing payment in a polite way
◇ Chasing payment in a serious way
◇ Learning tips for collecting money on time
◇ Understanding how to chase overdue payments

## Part 1  Practical Listening & Speaking

### A Word study

Work with your partner to fill in the blanks using the words on the left. Listen and check your answers, and then follow the recording.

| collect |
|---|
| chase payment |
| paid the invoice |
| Money is very tight |
| extension of credit |
| Overdraft |
| overheads |
| check |
| outstanding invoice |
| outstanding account |

(1) I'm sorry. _____ _____ _____ _____ at the moment.

(2) "Have you _____ _____ _____?" "I'm afraid we haven't."

(3) Could we ask for an _____ _____ _____? We are now going through a difficult period.

(4) We will _____ _____ _____ by the end of the month.

(5) When you _____ money from someone, you get money that you are owed.

(6) When you _____ _____, you urge someone to pay money to you.

(7) An _____ _____ is one which is not settled.

(8) An _____ _____ is one which is not paid.

(9) The firm _____ _____ before the building work was completed.

(10) If a payment is _____, it means that the money is not paid by the time expected.

174

| overdue |
|---|
| make the payment |
| went bankrupt |

(11) Their offices are in London, so the _____ are very high.

(12) _____ is the amount of money you owe to a bank when you have spent more money than you had in your account.

(13) Could you please send us a _____ before the end of the month?

## B Functional listening

*Task One (Chasing payment in a polite way):* Listen to the recording and fill in the blanks.

Ben: Good morning. Ben Wallace here.
Sue: Good morning, Mr. Wallace. This is Sue Anniston from KKL. (1) _____. Did you receive our June shipment?
Ben: Yes, we did. It arrived on the 24<sup>th</sup> of June.
Sue: Did you receive the invoice as well?
Ben: Yes, yes.
Sue: And (2) _____ for the last shipment yet?
Ben: I'm afraid we haven't managed that.
Sue: Because I haven't a record of the payment and our department was just getting a bit worried about it.
Ben: Yes, (3) _____ at the moment. I'd like to ask for an extension of credit.
Sue: Mmhmm.
Ben: You see, we have a big overdraft. And our overheads have to be thought about.
Sue: I see.
Ben: A major problem is that (4) _____ going through a difficult period too.
Sue: Yes, I know how that is.
Ben: So what do you suggest we do about the money we owe you?
Sue: Could you (5) _____ before the end of the month? That's one more week.
Ben: Yes, we will do our best.
Sue: I hope we can continue to cooperate together.
Ben: I hope so too.
Sue: And we hope to (6) _____ despite any troubles you may be having.
Ben: Thank you very much for being so understanding. Goodbye.

*Task Two* (*Chasing payment in a serious way*): Listen to the conversation and complete the following notes using one or two words from the recording.

(1) Mr. Dawson is calling about the outstanding _____ , which has been _____ for one month.

(2) Ms. Green should have made the payment on _____ _____ .

(3) Ms. Green's company has just given one of their major clients an _____ two weeks' _____ .

(4) Ms. Green's company has a large _____ with another customer who owes them a lot of money.

(5) Mr. Dawson would like the payment to be made _____ any more _____ .

## C Language check

Work with your partner to complete the following conversations. Then listen and check your answers.

*Task One: Chasing payment in a friendly way*

*Mentioning the invoice*

F: I'm sorry to ring you like this. Did you receive our last invoice?

M: Yes, we did.

F: Have you (1) _____ the invoice yet?

M: I'm afraid we haven't managed that.

*Mentioning the reasons for late payment*

F: Could you tell me when you can (2) _____ the payment?

M: I'm sorry. Money is very (3) _____ at the moment. We have a big overdraft, and our overheads have to be thought about.

F: I see.

M: A major problem is that our own (4) _____ are going through a difficult period too.

F: Yes, I know how that is.

*Asking for an extension of credit*

M: So could we ask for an (5) _____ of credit?

F: OK. Would you please make the payment by the end of this month? That's two more weeks.

*Promising to take action*

M: We'll (6) _____ you a check by the end of the month. Thank you for being so understanding.

F: You're welcome. We hope to keep you as a (7) _____ customer despite any troubles you may be having.

*Task Two: Chasing payment in a serious way*

*Chasing the invoice*

F: Did you receive our invoice?

M: Yes, we did.

F: Do you realize the payment has been (1) _____ for two months?

*Mentioning the reasons for late payment*

M: I'm sorry. We have a number of (2) _____ accounts ourselves. Besides, we have just given one of our major clients an extra two weeks' credit.

F: Yes, but our agreement was quite clear about the payment. You should (3) _____ paid us on August 5$^{th}$.

M: I'm really sorry. We have a large crisis with another customer who (4) _____ us a lot of money. They've just gone bankrupt.

*Insisting on prompt payment*

F: Anyway, we want you to settle the (5) _____ without any more delay. You know that you have exceeded your credit limit.

M: Yes. We'll try out best.

*Threatening to use legal action*

F: We need the payment immediately. I'm sure you don't want us to take legal (6) _____ .

M: Yes, of course. We'll send you the payment by the end of this week.

*Ending the call*

F: We look forward to the payment. Thank you. Goodbye.

M: Goodbye.

## D Controlled practice

You are a seller. Your partner is a buyer. Work together to make a dialogue based on the following flow chart. Listen to the recording of a model answer, and then follow it.

| YOU | YOUR PARTNER |
|---|---|
| Begin the call. | Respond. |
| Ask if the buyer received the invoice. | Say you received it. |
| Ask if the buyer has paid the invoice. | Say you haven't. Say there is an error in the invoice. |
| Apologize. Say you will send a new invoice right away. | Respond. |
| Ask when to make the payment. | Say you will make the payment as soon as you receive the new one. |
| Thank the buyer. | Respond and end the call. |

## E Business culture

Work with your partner to answer the following questions. Then listen to the recording and fill in the blanks.

(1) Have you ever collected money from a customer?
(2) What if your client failed to pay you on time?
(3) Do you have any effective ways of collecting payment?

---

### Tips for Collecting Money on Time

*Checking your customer's ability to pay*

Before you offer a customer (1) _____ , you should try to check their credit standing(资信状况) with other businesses(公司) or ask for their bank references(证明材料). Make these checks on a (2) _____ basis.

*Setting out your terms of trading*

Be specific about when you (3) _____ payment, for example, 30 days from the date of the invoice. Make sure your customer knows the (4) _____ before you do any work.

*Collecting your payment on time*

Remember to (5) _____ invoices promptly and collect the payment on time. If invoices are (6) _____ , spare no time to chase payment.

*Issuing correct invoices and keeping clear records*

Incorrect invoices or unclear records are among the main reasons for (7) _____ payment. Make sure you send correct invoices to the right person and the right (8) _____.

*Setting up a collection system*

When chasing payment, keep records of all correspondence（信函）and (9) _____. Give priority to your largest accounts, but chase the smaller amounts too. If a customer (10) _____ you a check and it doesn't arrive, chase it right away. If regular chasing does not produce (11) _____, consider stopping further supplies to the customer. If the payment is not obtained, ask a debt collector（讨债公司）or solicitor（律师）to collect the money for you.

# Part 2  Business Speaking

##  Pair work

**Task One:** The following 12 sentences are for chasing payment. Six of them are polite; the other six are impolite. Work with your partner to put them into the appropriate places in the table below. Then practice using the polite expressions.

(1) We don't want to take the matter any further.
(2) I'm looking forward to your early payment.
(3) We want you to make the payment without any more delay.
(4) I'm sorry to ring you like this.
(5) Would you please settle the account by the end of this week?
(6) You must know that our agreement was quite clear about payment.
(7) Could you tell me when you'll make the payment?
(8) May I remind you that payment is now overdue?
(9) Don't you know you have exceeded your credit limit?
(10) Could you please send us a check by the end of this month?
(11) We'll take legal action if you don't pay us this month.
(12) I don't think I like your attitude.

|  Polite Sentences |  Impolite Sentences |
|---|---|
|  |  |

***Task Two:*** The "paperwork" means the movement of documents involved in a transaction. The operations below are not in a logical order. Work together to put them in order by writing (1), (2), (3), etc. beside each operation. The first one has been done for you. Then take turns to describe the operations to each other.

| ( ) | A. You check the payment. |
|---|---|
| ( ) | B. The customer places an order. |
| ( ) | C. The customer checks the invoice. |
| ( ) | D. You acknowledge the order. |
| ( ) | E. You invoice the customer. |
| (1) | F. A potential customer makes an inquiry. |
| ( ) | G. You produce and dispatch the goods. |
| ( ) | H. You quote a selling price. |
| ( ) | I. The customer makes payment. |

## B Role play

***Task One:*** Look at the table below. There are some reasons for not paying an invoice on time. Work in pairs and take turns to practice a dialogue. Follow the example.

Unit 14

(1) The invoice was mislaid.
(2) I'm afraid we're rather short of cash.
(3) We also have outstanding accounts.
(4) The invoice was not received.
(5) The consignment was faulty.
(6) Our key client went bankrupt.
(7) We ordered 1,000 and you billed us for 1,500.
(8) We're still waiting for the rest of goods.
(9) Our finance people were on sick leave last week.

A: Can you tell me when you can make the payment?
B: I'm sorry. I've mislaid the invoice. Can you send me another one?

*Task Two:* Role-play a telephone conversation about chasing payment according to the following situations. You are a seller. Your partner is a buyer. After the practice, change roles.

A: Did you receive our last invoice?
B: Yes, we did.

*Information for you:*

You are responsible for Credit Control at Jeans House. Today is July 5th. Phone Robert Burton and explain that you are still waiting for payment of this invoice.

**Jeans House**
HOO FARM ESTATE, KIDDERMINSTER, WORCESTERSHIRE

Robert Burton
Rue de Livourne 15
1032 Brussels
BELGIUM

Invoice No.  : 34821
Date         : June 8th
Customer No. : 87663

| Item | No | Units | Price | Total |
| --- | --- | --- | --- | --- |
| Jeans | 4500-21 | 30 | $69 | $2,070 |

Payment within 30 days

*Information for your partner:*

You are Robert Burton. Today is July 5th. You will get a phone call about this invoice. Explain why you didn't make payment. Your reason is handwritten at the bottom of the invoice.

**Jeans House**
HOO FARM ESTATE, KIDDERMINSTER, WORCESTERSHIRE

Robert Burton
Rue de Livourne 15
1032 Brussels
BELGIUM

Invoice No. : 34821
Date : June 8$^{th}$
Customer No. : 87663

| Item | No | Units | Price | Total |
| --- | --- | --- | --- | --- |
| Jeans | 4500 - 21 | 30 | $ 69 | $ 2,070 |

Payment within 30 days
We ordered 10 of each, small, medium and large. They sent all small.

# Part 3  Listening Practice

## Ⓐ Listening focus

**Predicting while listening**

*Task One:* Listen to a story and choose the best answer to each question you hear.

(1) Why did the boy go to the coffee shop?
　　A. He went to look for his parents.
　　B. He wanted to have someone play with him.
　　C. He was hungry.
　　D. He wanted to have an ice cream.
(2) Why did the boy study the coins?
　　A. He was interested in them.
　　B. He had a habit of collecting coins.
　　C. He was afraid if he had enough coins to buy an ice cream.
　　D. He was eager to have an ice cream.
(3) What did the boy order?

A. A plain ice cream. B. An ice cream sundae.
C. Some coins. D. A bill.

(4) What did the boy do when he finished the ice cream?

A. He paid the cashier and departed.

B. He put some changes on the table, paid the cashier and departed.

C. He paid the bill and left.

D. He put some money on the dish and departed.

(5) What do you think the money the boy left was for?

A. He forgot to take.

B. He didn't want them.

C. He left the money as a tip to the waitress.

D. He wanted to buy another ice cream.

*Task Two:* You will hear some sentences. They are the first sentences of some passages. Choose the best answer which indicates your prediction of the possible topic of each short passage.

(1) What are the experiments?

A. Experiments to find out how clever monkeys were.

B. Experiments to test the intelligence of different animals.

C. Experiments to compare the differences between man and the monkey.

D. Experiments to find out how monkeys searched for food.

(2) What will be the main topic of the talk?

A. Library regulations. B. Location of the library.
C. Use of library facilities. D. Library personnel.

(3) What will the passage be mainly about?

A. The proper relationship between professors and students.

B. The classroom environment in universities.

C. The social position of university teachers.

D. The friendship between students and their professors.

(4) What will the speaker mainly talk about?

A. The loneliness of some people.

B. The family problem.

C. The importance and real meaning of friendship.

D. The relationship between friends.

(5) What will the passage be about?

A. Children's acquisition of the mother tongue.

B. Ways of teaching babies to talk.

C. Differences between a child's language and an adult's.

D. The importance of learning foreign languages.

## B Dictation

*Task One:* Listen to the short passage twice and fill in the blanks with the missing words or sentences.

My name is Steven Brown. I live in Detroit and own a small factory with more than 100 employees (1) _____ laptop computer accessories. And I also offer computer (2) _____ services for individuals and businesses including Web hosting, network development, Internet (3) _____ , e-commerce, and customer software support, etc. I have been (4) _____ my own business for over eight years and to date no client has defaulted on paying me for work done. However, on (5) _____ I still have to spend time in chasing customers for invoices that are 2 or 3 months old. I really don't enjoy doing this for (6) _____ . I try to avoid it by agreeing terms up front and by sending statements as well as invoices (some businesses seem to only pay on statements). (7) _____ , but still in vain. Now I'm quite puzzled and wondering (8) _____ to encourage earlier payment that will not harm my client relationships.

*Task Two:* You're going to hear five sentences. Repeat each sentence you hear. Then listen again and write down each sentence. Check your answer when you listen for the third time.

(1) _____
(2) _____
(3) _____
(4) _____
(5) _____

## C Conversations

**Conversation 1**

*Task One:* Listen to the conversation and number the following in sequence. The fourth one has been done for you.

A. Ms. Evans complains about the delayed payment to the secretary.
B. The secretary tells Julia Evans that Mr. Simon is not available.
C. Julia Evans makes the telephone and wants to speak to Mr. Davy Simon.
D. Ms. Evans threatens to take legal action against Mr. Simon's company.
E. The secretary promises to call Mr. Simon immediately and let him call back to Ms. Evans.
F. The secretary admits that her company has an unexpected cash flow gap problem.

*Task Two:* Listen to the conversation again and complete the message below.

```
                    Blueberry (1) _____
 ┌─────────────────────┐
 │ WHILE YOU WERE OUT  │
 └─────────────────────┘
 To:      Davy Simon        Date:          1st Oct.
 From:    Julia Evans       Company:  (2) Q. A. C. Export Co. Ltd.

 ┌─────────┐
 │ MESSAGE │
 └─────────┘

 She wants to talk to you directly.
 She is ringing about (3) _____ .
 She complains that (4) _____ is still not allocated.
 Call back to her (5) _____ .
```

## Conversation 2

*Task One:* Listen to the conversation and decide whether the following sentences are true (T) or false (F).

(1) The relationship between Amanda and Bob is boss and assistant. (　)
(2) Amanda calls Bob to complain about the bad service she has received. (　)
(3) Amanda makes an apology for not paying enough attention to the matter. (　)
(4) Bob tells Amanda he used to work in a bigger organization. (　)
(5) Amanda hopes the accident won't affect their future business. (　)

*Task Two:* Listen to the conversation again and answer the following questions.

(1) When did Bob send Amanda a fax?

(2) Why didn't Amanda respond to the fax?

(3) Why don't bigger organizations worry about cash flow difficulties according to Bob?

(4) How much is unpaid?

(5) What will Amanda do the first thing in the afternoon?

## D Passage

*Task One:* Listen to the passage and choose the best answer to each of the following questions.

(1) What is the passage mainly about?
   A. How to take legal action against someone.
   B. How to complain of overdue payments.
   C. How to do business on the Internet.
   D. How to chase overdue payments.

(2) What aspect of doing business does the speaker hate most?
   A. To extract payments from customers and write some of it off as a bad debt.
   B. To spend so much time in e-commerce and, in the end, get no pay at all.
   C. To respond to an email within 24 hours and call people by phone.
   D. To take legal action over debt by using the court system whenever possible.

(3) What should you do if a client says the payment will be made by Wednesday?
   A. Follow them up on a Wednesday morning.
   B. Follow them up on a Wednesday evening.
   C. Follow them up on a Tuesday evening.
   D. Follow them up on a Thursday morning.

(4) Which sentence is TRUE according to the passage?
   A. Chasing overdue payments is quite indecent nowadays.
   B. Chasing overdue payments is not boring as most think.
   C. Chasing overdue payments is tedious and stressful.
   D. Chasing overdue payments is very easy and exciting.

(5) What does the sentence "An ounce of prevention is worth a pound of cure" mean?
   A. People should take action to prevent the possible occurrence of overdue payment.
   B. People should try their best not to be cheated by those non-paying partners and clients.
   C. No solution has been found yet to prevent undesirable consequence of overdue payment.
   D. Using the court system proves to be the most useful way to collect overseas debt.

*Task Two:* Listen to the passage again and fill in the blanks with the missing information.

Author's suggestions:
- It is advisable to use (1) _____.
- If you collect debt yourself, you should have (2) _____ of the debt together.

186 | Unit 14  When can you make the payment

- Any emails that refer to (3) _____ should be brought out.
- Keep notes on every phone call or email you make in relation to the debt.
- Following up payment is especially important if the debt is held by (4) _____ _____.
- If they don't respond to an email within 24 hours, you should (5) _____ _____.
- Don't threaten to take legal action over debt easily.
- An ounce of prevention is worth a pound of cure.

## Part 4  Fun Listening

*Task One:* Listen to the story "Parking Expenses" and tell the funny part to the class.

### Parking Expenses

A businessman walked into a New York City bank and asked for the loan officer. He said he was going to Europe on business for two weeks and needed to borrow $5,000. The loan officer said the bank would need some security for such a loan. The businessman then handed over the keys to a Rolls Royce that was parked on the street in front of the bank. Everything was checked out and the loan officer accepted the car as collateral for the loan. An employee then drove the Rolls into the bank's underground garage and parked it there.

Two weeks later the businessman returned, repaid the $5,000 and the interest which came to $15.41. The loan officer said, "We do appreciate your business and this transaction has worked out very nicely, but we are a bit puzzled. While you were away we checked and found that you are a multimillionaire. What puzzles us is why you would bother to borrow $5,000?"

The businessman replied: "Where else in New York City can I park my car for 2 weeks for 15 bucks?"

# Unit 15　I'm sorry to hear that

Unit Goals
◇ Making a complaint
◇ Dealing with a complaint
◇ Learning tips for making and dealing with complaints
◇ Taking notes while listening

## Part 1　Practical Listening & Speaking

### A Word study

Work with your partner to fill in the blanks using the words on the left. Listen and check your answers, and then follow the recording.

| make a complaint |
| Consignment |
| slip-up |
| refund |
| dispatcher |
| inconvenience |
| look into |
| is concerned with |
| swivel chairs |
| short delivery |
| sort out |

(1) The problem _____ _____ _____ our last order.
(2) I'm phoning to _____ _____ _____ about the faulty goods we received from you.
(3) When you _____ _____ a problem, you try to find out the truth about it in order to solve it.
(4) When you _____ _____ a problem, you successfully deal with it.
(5) This is the second time we have received a _____ _____.
(6) We placed an order for 45 _____ _____, but only 40 arrived.
(7) A _____ _____ is a maintenance team.
(8) I think the goods must've been damaged _____ _____.
(9) A _____ is a careless mistake.
(10) A _____ is a state or an instance of confusion.
(11) We asked you to pack the goods in _____ _____, but you packed them in cardboard boxes.

188

| in transit |
| metal containers |
| mix-up |
| service team |

(12) _____ is a quantity of goods that are sent somewhere, especially in order to be sold.

(13) We apologize for the delay and any _____ caused.

(14) When you _____ someone, you give him or her back money.

(15) A _____ is someone who is in charge of sending goods.

## B Functional listening

*Task One (Making a complaint):* Listen to the recording and fill in the blanks.

Sue: DND Office Furniture. Can I help you?

Don: Oh, hello. This is Don Jackson from PC Solutions. Could I speak to Sue Lee (1) _____?

Sue: Sue Lee speaking. How may I help you, Mr. Jackson?

Don: I'm phoning about our last order. I'm afraid there's a bit of a problem with it.

Sue: Oh, dear. (2) _____?

Don: Well, it was two weeks late for a start. When we received the consignment, we found part of it was missing.

Sue: Oh, dear. (3) _____. Could I have the order number, please?

Don: It's BN567233.

Sue: BN567233. I'll just check that. Mr. Jackson, I'm afraid there may be a slip-up in our dispatch department.

Don: When can we (4) _____? It's essential that we have them by the end of the month.

Sue: I'm very sorry. I'll call the dispatcher immediately and get back to you as soon as possible.

Don: But I need to know (5) _____. I'll have to cancel if we don't receive it by the end of the month.

Sue: I'm sorry for the delay and any inconvenience caused. I'll look into it as soon as possible. Could I have your phone number? I'll (6) _____.

Don: OK. It's 5433,5644.

Sue: 5433,5644. Right, Mr. Jackson. I'll see what I can do.

Don: Thanks. Goodbye.

Sue: Goodbye.

> **Task Two (Dealing with a complaint)**: Listen to the conversation and complete the following notes using one or two words from the recording.

(1) The man says he ordered 27 swivel chairs, but only _____ have arrived.

(2) The man says it's the second time that they have received a _____ _____.

(3) The woman says that their dispatcher misread the number on the _____ _____.

(4) The man says the delay is causing them problems with _____ _____.

(5) The woman _____ the man that this kind of thing will not happen again.

## ❸ Language check

> Work with your partner to complete the following conversations and expressions. Then listen and check your answers.

**Task One: Making and dealing with a complaint**

*Opening the call*

F: OTC Office Furniture. Can I help you?

M: Oh, hello. This is James Bond (1) _____ ABC Partnership. Could I speak to Mary Sung in the Sales?

*Offering help*

F: Mary Sung speaking. (2) _____ can I do for you, Mr. Bond?

M: I'm phoning (3) _____ our last order. I'm afraid there's a bit of a problem with it.

*Asking about the problem*

F: Oh, dear. What (4) _____ is the problem?

M: Well, it was one week late for a start. When we received the goods, we found part of it was missing.

*Asking for the order number*

F: Oh, dear. I'm sorry to (5) _____ that. Could I have the order number, please?

190 | Unit 15  *I'm sorry to hear that*

M: It's BN567233.

*Finding out the reason*

F: BN567233. I'll just check that. Mr. Bond, I'm (6) _____ there may be a slip-up in our shipping department.

M: When can we (7) _____ the rest of the order? It's important that we have them by the end of the month.

*Apologizing and promising to take action*

F: I'm sorry for the delay and any inconvenience caused. I'll call the dispatcher immediately and get (8) _____ to you as soon as possible. Could I have your phone number?

M: OK. It's 5433,5644.

F: 5433,5644. Right, Mr. Bond. I'll call you back in a minute.

*Ending the call*

M: Thanks. Goodbye.

F: Goodbye.

## Task Two: *Making a complaint*

*Delivery*

- I'm calling about our last consignment. It was four days late.
- I'm (1) _____ about our last order. You sent us the wrong size of desks.
- When we received the consignment, we found (2) _____ of it was missing.

*Quality and packing of goods*

- The quality of the goods doesn't (3) _____ to be Class A, which is what we ordered.
- The outer packing was wrong: you packed them in plastic boxes (4) _____ of metal containers we asked for. As a result, 700 units were damaged.

*Services*

- I'm calling about the performance of your service team.
- The engineer refused to service the old computer. We were very disappointed (5) _____ your services.

*Payment*

- The total was $40,000, but you only sent us $35,000. Can you send us the (6) _____ immediately?

- I've checked the account and you still owe us $15,000.
- The invoice should have been (7) _____ a month ago.

**Task Three: Dealing with a complaint**

*Asking for information*

- Could I (1) _____ who's calling, please?
- Could I have the order number, please?
- Could you tell me your phone number?

*Clarifying*

- I'm sorry. Could you repeat the problem?
- Can you (2) _____ on while I make a note of that? Did you say the shipment was delayed for one week?
- Let me (3) _____ if I've got that. Did you say that the goods were lost in transit?
- Let me just run through that again. Did you say some of the goods were damaged in transit?

*Accepting responsibility and explaining the reason*

- Please accept our apologies. It's certainly our (4) _____.
- We're very sorry. We're having trouble with our suppliers.
- I'm (5) _____ sorry. There is a slip-up in our shipping department.

*Denying responsibility*

- I'm sorry, but I don't think we can help you solve the problem.
- I see the (6) _____, but this is not our fault.
- I understand the problem, but this is not really our responsibility.

*Playing for time*

- I'll see what I can do.
- Please (7) _____ it with me.
- I'll check the records and then get back to you tomorrow.
- Can I get back to you tomorrow?

*Promising to take action*

- I'll arrange a replacement (8) _____ away.
- I'll contact our factory right away and ask them to send you the parts.
- I'll have to check this (9) _____ my boss, and send you the payment.
- We'll refund your money immediately.

## D Controlled practice

You are a seller. Your partner is a buyer. Work together to make a telephone dialogue based on the following prompts. Listen to the recording of a model answer, and then follow it.

| YOU | YOUR PARTNER |
|---|---|
| Open the talk by greeting. | Greet and introduce yourself. |
| Greet him/her and offer help. | Say there is a problem about your last order. |
| Ask about the problem. | Say the quality of the goods is not Class A. |
| Say there's a slip-up in your shipping department. Apologize and ask what to do with the goods. | Say you can keep the goods if there is a 20% discount and ask them to ship Class A right away. |
| Agree to ship tomorrow. | Say that's fine. |
| Apologize again. | Respond. |

## E Business culture

Work with your partner to answer the following questions. Then listen to the recording and fill in the blanks.

(1) Have you ever made a complaint? What was the result?
(2) Have you ever dealt with a complaint? What was the result?
(3) What should you pay attention to when you make or deal with a complaint?

### Tips for Making and Dealing with a Complaint

Making and dealing with complaints is very (1) _____ in business practice. Here are some tips for you to make and deal with a complaint.

*Making a complaint*
*Preparations:* Before you make a complaint, you should prepare for the call. Make sure you have all the (2) _____ in front of you. Also decide what you (3) _____ to solve the problem.

*Talking to the person responsible:* As a general rule, you should complain to the right person who is responsible for the (4) _____. If you do not know who is responsible, make a call first to (5) _____ out who is responsible.

*Speaking clearly:* Summarize your complaint as best as you can. Use no more than three sentences to make your (6) _____ clear and simple. There is no need to go into great (7) _____, as the other person may be confused or can't remember what you say.

*Being firm but polite*: Do not take offence(生气) when you are complaining. (8) _____ goes a long way in getting other people's help to meet your (9) _____. Being angry would only make you unprofessional. It will not help (10) _____ the problem, but only lead to more frustration(挫折) and anger.

*Asking for action*: Ask what (11) _____ you wish the other side to take to resolve your problem. If you do not get what you want, keep control and state what you need (12) _____. Don't use threats unless you have to.

*Dealing with a complaint*:
When you receive a complaint, you should consider your company's (13) _____. So always remain polite and patient. Don't (14) _____ the speaker when he/she is describing the problem. Express (15) _____ and say sorry after you hear what the caller says. Ask for the details of the problem, (16) _____ them down and repeat what you have written. If you are not following, ask the speaker to (17) _____ _____ and repeat the details. Accept responsibility if it's your fault. Then make reasonable suggestions, and promise to take action.

# Part 2  Business Speaking

## A Pair work

*Task One:* Read the telephone conversation below. Work with your partner to put it into correct order, and then practice it.

(1) May I help you?

(2) Do you have the receipt (收据)?

(3) I'm sorry, but the store policy is that we must have a receipt in order to refund your money.

(4) I'm sorry. He's not available right now.

A. Then who else is in charge in this store?

B. I want to speak to the manager about this, as I am very unhappy with this product.

C. Yes. I bought this answering machine two weeks ago and it hasn't worked properly since I bought it.

D. No, I didn't keep it.

**Task Two:** Student A is a buyer. Student B is a shop assistant. Student A bought a printer 3 days ago, but it's broken now. Work in pairs to complete the following dialogue with the help of the hints in the brackets, and then practice the dialogue.

A: Good morning.

A: I bought this printer three days ago, but it's broken now.

A: I prefer a replacment.

A: It's alright. Thank you for your help.

B: _____ (Greet him and offer help.)

B: _____ (Apologize. offer a refund or a replacement).

B: _____ (Provide a new one. Apologize again.)

B: _____ (End the talk.)

## B Role play

**Task One:** You are a seller. Your partner is a buyer. The buyer placed an order with you and is still waiting for the shipment, which has been late for one week. Work together to role-play a dialogue based on the following points.

| YOU | YOUR PARTNER |
|---|---|
| Answer the phone. | Greet him/her, and introduce yourself. |
| Greet him/her, and offer help. | Say you haven't received the order, which has been late for one week. |
| Ask for the order number. | Give the order number: HNJ4566. |
| Apologize. Say you have a problem with your supplier. | Respond. Ask when you can have the goods. |
| Say you will check with the shipping department and call him/her back. Apologize again. | Respond and finish the call. |

**Task Two:** Read the following answering machine message from a customer. To deal with his/her complaint, make a call to him/her. Take turns in playing each role in the conversation. Follow this example.

A: Hello. This is Rose Jones. Could I speak to Max Matt, please?
B: Max Matt speaking. Hi, Ms. Jones, how are you?

Hello. This is Max Matt from PPL International in Australia. We've just accepted delivery of a consignment of A44 motors. Unfortunately, there were no operating instructions included. Could you send us them as soon as possible? Thanks.

# Part 3 Listening Practice

## A Listening focus

### Taking Notes While Listening

**Task One:** You are going to hear a bus schedule. Listen carefully and fill in the chart with what you hear.

| Bus Schedule | | | |
|---|---|---|---|
| Destination | Departure Time | Arrival Time | Fare |
| (1) Reno, NV | _____ | _____ | $ 98.00 |
| (2) Fresno, CA | _____ | 1:45 p.m. | $ 62.00 |
| (3) Seattle, WA | 8:30 a.m. | _____ | _____ |
| (4) Boise, ID | 10:40 a.m. | _____ | _____ |

**Task Two:** Listen to the following telephone conversation between a shop assistant of an electronic store and his customer. Fill in the order ticket according to what you hear.

M: Hello!
F: May I speak to Mr. Golden, please?
M: Speaking.
F: Good morning, Mr. Golden. This is Mary Thomson from INA Industries. Our

196 | Unit 15 *I'm sorry to hear that*

company is going to buy 3 PIV model computers.

M: 256K on hard drive models or 256k optional on base models?

F: Have you got any suggestions?

M: The kind of 40G on hard drive models are suitable for general use. And the 40G optional on base models is available upon request. It's a bit more expensive.

F: I think I will buy the former, 40G hard drive model.

M: OK! When do you want them? We have this computer in stock.

F: That's fine. I hope the computers will arrive on Friday morning.

M: Friday morning. Where is your company located?

F: No. 21 Rose Street, near the Fashion Store.

M: And your telephone number is...?

F: 72188155. Thank you.

M: Thank you for your business.

---

Order Ticket (Spring Electronic Store)
9:30 a.m. 20th June D. Golden

**Information of Customer**
Name              Mary Thomson
Company           _____
Address           _____
Telephone Number  _____

**Information of Computers**
Type              PIV models _____ on hard drive
Quantity          _____
Delivery Date     _____

---

## B Dictation

*Task One:* Listen to the short passage twice and fill in the blanks with the missing words or sentences.

The airline lost your baggage. The hotel laundry (1) _____ your favorite shirt. The taxi driver (2) _____ you. When you're abroad, sometimes things go wrong. Now you can do something about it! Use these tips when you want to express an (3) _____ complaint in English.

No matter how unfair the situation, it's best to phrase your complaint politely. In English, you'll sound more polite if you use (4) _____ language. Here are some examples:

*Can you help me with this?*

Everyone would much rather be asked to do something than told! So try

(5) _____ your complaint as a request for help: "Can you help me with this?
(6) _____."

*I'm afraid there may be a misunderstanding.*

This is a polite way of saying, "Your information is wrong. Please fix it now."
(7) _____ if you made reservations for a flight, hotel or restaurant, and when you arrive, it's not what you expected. For instance, "I'm afraid there may be a misunderstanding. (8) _____."

*Task Two:* You're going to hear five sentences. Repeat each sentence you hear. Then listen again and write down each sentence. Check your answer when you listen for the third time.

(1) _____
(2) _____
(3) _____
(4) _____
(5) _____

## ◉ Conversations

**Conversation 1**

*Task One:* Listen to the conversation and choose the best answer to each question you hear.

(1) Where does this conversation most likely take place?
   A. In a park.                      B. In a restaurant.
   C. At a birthday party.            D. In a shop.
(2) What is the most probable relationship between the two speakers?
   A. Teacher and student.            B. Classmates.
   C. Customer and shop-assistant.    D. Supervisor and subordinator.
(3) When was the watch bought?
   A. One week ago.                   B. Two weeks ago.
   C. Three weeks ago.                D. Four weeks ago.
(4) Which of the following statement is true?
   A. The alarm doesn't work and the strap leaves a green mark on the wrist.
   B. The alarm doesn't work and the watch is beyond guarantee.
   C. The strap leaves a green mark on the wrist but the watch is beyond guarantee.
   D. The price was much higher in this shop.
(5) How was the complaint dealt with?
   A. A refund was given.

198 | Unit 15  *I'm sorry to hear that*

B. The watch was replaced.

C. The watch was fixed.

D. Nothing was done about it.

**Task Two:** Listen to the conversation again and write down the five questions asked by the shop assistant.

(1) _____

(2) _____

(3) _____

(4) _____

(5) _____

## Conversation 2

**Task One:** Listen to the conversation and choose the best answer to each question.

(1) Where does this conversation most likely take place?
   A. In a park.               B. In a restaurant.
   C. At a hotel.              D. In a shop.

(2) What do you think the man is?
   A. A shop-assistant.        B. The woman's subordinator.
   C. The woman's friend.      D. A waiter.

(3) What is the matter according to the woman?
   A. The light is too bright and the room is too hot.
   B. The light is too bright and the room is too cold.
   C. The light is too dim and the room is too hot.
   D. The light is too dim and the room is too cold.

(4) How does the man deal with the problem concerning the "cold" room?
   A. Turn on the air-conditioner.
   B. Turn off the air-conditioner.
   C. Bring in a heater.
   D. Bring in a blanket and some hot water.

(5) What can we learn from the conversation?
   A. The woman is out of reason.
   B. The woman is impolite.
   C. The woman is not well.
   D. The woman is sleepy.

*Task Two:* Listen to the conversation again and write down the things the man does for the woman.

(1) _____

(2) _____

(3) _____

(4) _____

## D Passage

*Task One:* Listen to the passage and decide whether the following statements are true (T) or false (F).

(1) The man's telephone has been out of service for ten days. (    )
(2) The man's telephone has been out of service due to the failure of payment. (    )
(3) The man made a phone call to the Complaints Department and got a satisfactory answer. (    )
(4) The girl in the Complaints Department was very rude. (    )
(5) The man asked for a formal apology from the girl. (    )

*Task Two:* Listen to the passage again and complete the answer to the following question.

What does the man require in the letter?
The girl in question should be disciplined, and instructed _____.
And he hopes she can make _____ to him.

# Part 4  Fun Listening

*Task One:* Listen to the song "You'll Be In My Heart" and sing along.

### Phil Collins — You'll Be In My Heart — "Tarzan"

Come stop your crying
It will be all right
Just take my hand hold it tight

I will protect you
from all around you

I will be here
Don't you cry

For one so small,
you seem so strong
My arms will hold you,

keep you safe and warm
This bond between us
Can't be broken
I will be here
Don't you cry

'Cause you'll be in my heart
Yes, you'll be in my heart
From this day on
Now and forever more

You'll be in my heart
No matter what they say
You'll be here in my heart, always

Why can't they understand
the way we feel
They just don't trust
what they can't explain
I know we're different but,
deep inside us
We're not that different at all

And you'll be in my heart
Yes, you'll be in my heart
From this day on

Now and forever more

Don't listen to them
'Cause what do they know
We need each other,
to have, to hold
They'll see in time
I know

When destiny calls you
You must be strong
I may not be with you
But you've got to hold on
They'll see in time
I know
We'll show them together

'Cause you'll be in my heart
Yes, you'll be in my heart
From this day on,
Now and forever more

Oh, you'll be in my heart
No matter what they say
You'll be in my heart, always
Always

# Unit 16 How was the last order

## Unit Goals
◇ Calling a previous client
◇ Describing the sales trend
◇ Learning 5 tips for a successful sales call
◇ Learning lessons from an ineffective sales call

## Part 1  Practical Listening & Speaking

### A Word study

Work with your partner to fill in the blanks using the words on the left. Listen and check your answers, and then follow the recording.

| booth |
| convention |
| fabulous |
| prospective |
| come by |
| in person |
| reached a peak |
| hit rock-bottom |
| static |
| fluctuates |
| In the run-up to |
| rocketed |

(1) _____ _____ _____ _____ Christmas, sales jumped from $650,000 to $1.2 million.
(2) Sales _____ _____ _____ in October.
(3) Sales _____ _____ in June.
(4) If you do something _____ _____, you do it yourself.
(5) Generally, the _____ _____ of last year was satisfactory.
(6) There was a _____ _____ in sales from June to September.
(7) I'll _____ _____ the house and get my stuff later, OK?
(8) Economists predict that housing prices will remain _____ for a long period.
(9) _____, prices are still rising.
(10) Car sales _____ from 180 to 2,000 last year.
(11) If a price or an amount _____, it keeps changing and becoming higher and lower.
(12) A _____ client is someone who is likely to buy things from you soon.

| Overall sales performance | (13) A _____ change means a great and sudden change. |
| --- | --- |
| | (14) A _____ is a small partly enclosed structure where you can buy things or get information, usually at a market or a trade fair. |
| gradual/steady decline | (15) A _____ is a large formal meeting for people who belong to the same profession or organization or who have the same interests. |
| dramatic | (16) The room has _____ views across the lake. |

## B Functional listening

*Task One (Calling a previous client):* Listen to the recording and fill in the blanks.

Dan: Hello, this is Dan Williams from KLP International. Could I speak to Karen Henderson?

Karen: Hello, this is Karen. How may I help you, Dan?

Dan: Hi, Karen. How is everything at Fun Games?

Karen: Just fine. How are you doing?

Dan: I'm doing very well. You know, recently I read in the *Business Times* that Fun Games has done very well since you had (1) _____.

Karen: Actually, we've had a fabulous year. And the convention was a huge success.

Dan: Great, I'm glad to hear it! I'd like to inform you that next year's convention has already been scheduled. The booths go pretty quickly.

Karen: (2) _____ as soon as possible, right?

Dan: Yes, of course! What do you think? Will Fun Games be interested in displaying products for thousands of prospective customers to see?

Karen: I don't know, Dan. (3) _____ at the convention center in Allen Town are one-quarter of the price as those here in Jack Town.

Dan: Of course they are, Karen. But historically, many more buyers (4) _____ in Jack Town.

Karen: You may be right, but people are traveling longer distances to these things nowadays.
Dan: Could I (5) _____ so that I can discuss this with you in person?
Karen: Well, I suppose I could meet with you after lunch. How about two p.m.?
Dan: Great. See you then.

*Task Two (Describing the sales trend)*: Listen to the recording and check (√) *True* or *False*.

|  | True | False |
|---|---|---|
| (1) The sales volume at the beginning of the year was very high. | ☐ | ☐ |
| (2) The sales volume in April was $300,000, which increased gradually to $650,000 in July. | ☐ | ☐ |
| (3) Between July and September, there was no big change in the sales. | ☐ | ☐ |
| (4) Just before Christmas, the sales reached a peak, which was $1.2 million. | ☐ | ☐ |

## ❸ Language check

Work with your partner to complete the following conversations. Then listen and check your answers.

### Task One: Calling a previous client

*Asking to speak to someone*

F: This is Susan Jones. May I speak to Stephen Davis?
M: This is Stephen Davis. (1) _____ may I help you, Ms. Jones?

*Making small talk*

F: Hi, Mr. Davis. How are (2) _____ there?
M: Pretty good, thanks. How about you?

*Asking about the quality*

F: I'm fine, thanks. How was the last order? Were you (3) _____ with the quality of our product?
M: Yes, they seemed OK. As you said, the quality of your product was (4) _____ standard.

*Asking about after-sales services*

F: That's good to hear. How about our after-sales service? Did our people (5) _____ you with good service?

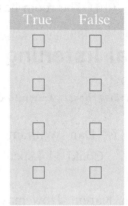
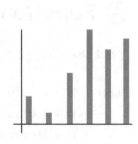

M: Yes, they did. And also they were very efficient.

*Asking for feedback*

F: Thanks. After using the product for a while, do you have any feedback (6) _____ the product?

M: Everything is fine at the moment.

*Asking for a new order*

F: Well, I was also wondering (7) _____ you might be interested in ordering another machine. It's our latest model.

M: That (8) _____ interesting. Could you send us the product description first?

*Ending the call*

F: Sure. I'll send it to you right away. I'm looking forward to your new (9) _____. Thank you for your time.

M: My pleasure. We'll get (10) _____ to you soon.

## Task Two: Describing the sales trend

*The general trend*

F: So how were the sales of last year?

M: Overall, the sales (1) _____ of last year was quite satisfactory.

*The highest*

F: In which month of last year did the sales (2) _____ a peak?

M: The sales peaked at $900,000 in May.

*The lowest*

F: In which month of last year did the sales hit rock-bottom?

M: The sales hit rock-bottom in January. The (3) _____ was $200,000.

*Sharp increase*

F: How were the sales from January to May?

M: The sales increased (rose) rapidly (dramatically) (4) _____ $200,000 to $900,000 in this period.

*Sharp decrease*

F: How were the sales after May?

M: There was a sudden (sharp) decline (drop) in sales from $900,000 to $600,000 (5) _____ May and July.

*Slight changes*

F: How were the sales between July and September?
M: The sales fluctuated (6) _____ $600,000 during these two months.

*Steady growth*

F: How were the sales of the last three months?
M: The last three months (7) _____ a steady (gradual) increase in sales, which went up from $600,000 to $700,000.

## D Controlled practice

You are a buyer. Your partner is a seller. Work together to make a dialogue based on the following prompts. Listen to the recording of a model answer, and then follow it.

| YOU | YOUR PARTNER |
|---|---|
| Ask about the product range. | Say you can offer a wide range of models. Model 345 is the latest. |
| Ask about the features of Model 345. | Say the model is very lightweight and durable. |
| Ask about the quality. | Say the quality is above standard. |
| Ask about the material. | Say it's made of imported materials. |

## E Business culture

Work with your partner to answer the following questions. Then listen to the recording and fill in the blanks.

(1) Have you ever made a sales call? How was the result?
(2) What is the most difficult part of a sales call? How can you keep the prospective client interested and on the line longer?

# Unit 16

### 5 Tips for a Successful Sales Call

A. Develop a professional greeting. Don't just say hello and (1) _____ _____ your telephone presentation without taking a breath. Begin with Mr., Mrs. or Ms, as in "Good morning, Mr. Smith." Or "Good evening, Mrs. Jones." Everyone else says, "Hello." Be (2) _____. Be (3) _____.

B. Introduce yourself and your company. "My name is John Smith with ABC Company. We're a local firm that (4) _____ in helping businesses like yours save money." Don't get too (5) _____ yet. Don't mention your product. If you do, that allows the other party to say, "Oh, we're happy with what we've got. Thanks anyway," and hang up. By keeping your introduction general, yet (6) _____ _____ _____, you'll keep them on the line longer.

C. Express thanks. Always thank the (7) _____ client for allowing you a few moments in his busy day. Tell him that you won't waste a second of his time. "I want to thank you for taking my call. This will only (8) _____ a moment of your time so you can get back to your busy (9) _____." Don't say that you'll "just take a moment."

D. State the purpose of your call. It's best if you can (10) _____ the purpose within a question. "If we can show you a way to improve the quality of your product at a (11) _____ _____, would you be interested to know more?" This is very likely to get a yes response. At this point, you're ready to start (12) _____ _____ _____ to meet this person or to get their permission to provide them with more information.

E. Schedule a meeting. Get a confirmation to meet him or her in order to give a good (13) _____. Offer him two times, "Mr. Johnson, I can come by your office at 2:15 p.m. today to discuss this further. Or would 9:45 a.m. tomorrow better (14) _____ _____ _____?" Thank them for their time today and for the upcoming appointment. Reconfirm the date, time and (15) _____ of the appointment. You may send a letter or an e-mail to confirm the visit. Keep it short and upbeat(乐观的).

# Part 2  Business Speaking

## A  Pair work

*Task One:* Use the expressions on the left below to label the pictures about the sales trend on the right. Then take turns to describe the pictures. Follow this example.

A: How were the sales according to Picture A?
B: The sales fell rapidly.

(1) increase steeply, reach a peak, and dropped drastically    A.

(2) remain steady    B.

(3) fall rapidly    C.

(4) rise gradually    D.

(5) increase steadily and level off    E.

(6) drop dramatically and recover    F.

*Task Two:* Complete the sentences using one of the following prepositions. Then take turns to say the sentences.

in    at    by    from    of    to

(1) Last year there was a drop _____ net sales _____ 9%.
(2) Market share increased _____ 3% up to 8%.
(3) Net sales peaked _____ $23 million in 2007.
(4) European sales went down _____ $4 million _____ $3 million.
(5) Sales leveled off _____ $6 million in 2007.
(6) Costs rose _____ $3.3 million. This was a rise _____ 10%.
(7) Office software sales fell _____ 10% in 2007.
(8) A strong euro meant a fall _____ exports in 2007.

# B Role play

*Task One:* Take turns to compare the sales of this year with those of last year. Follow this example.

A: How were the sales of this year in Brazil?
B: There was a decrease in sales from 1,070 of last year to 950 of this year.

|  | Last year | This year |
|---|---|---|
| Brazil | 1,070 | 950 |
| Iran | 470 | 470 |
| France | 50 | 470 |
| Singapore | 0 | 300 |
| Sweden | 360 | 290 |
| Peru | 150 | 220 |

*Task Two:* Take turns to describe the sales performance in the following graphs. Use the expressions provided.

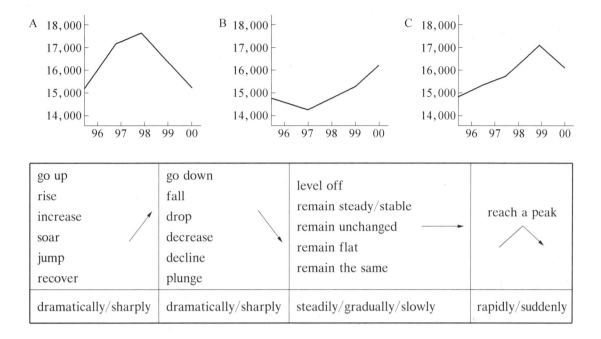

## Part 3 Listening Practice

### A Listening focus

**Summarizing While Listening**

*Task One:* Listen to a passage about student visas and match each kind of visa in Column A with its qualified applicants in Column B and the time of validity in Column C according to what you hear on the tape.

| A | B | C |
|---|---|---|
| F - 1 | exchange students | for the amount of time of the educational program plus an additional 60 days |
| M - 1 | students in universities | before applying for a different visa, they must return to his or her home country for at least two years |
| J - 1 | students in vocational institutions | for the period of time of the course plus 30 days or one year, whichever is less |

**Task Two:** Listen to a passage about climate in the United States, then summarize the weather in each part of the United States by putting all the items from A to F in the boxes below.

A. Hot in summer.
B. Cold in winter.
C. The temperature in summer and winter is not very different.
D. Summers are extremely hot and winters are extremely cold.
E. Quite warm in spring.
F. Rather cool in autumn.

| On the west coast | In the eastern states | In north central states |
|---|---|---|
|  |  |  |

## B Dictation

**Task One:** Listen to the short passage twice and fill in the blanks with the missing words or sentences.

A sales call shouldn't be something that happens by accident; it should be a planned (1) _____. When sales calls aren't planned, they often result in wasted time and effort, (2) _____ in a no sale. No matter how hard you try, you can't make a sale on every call but, as a minimum, you should be either starting a sale, moving a sale along, or trying to (3) _____ one.
I'm talking about sales calls here, not (4) _____ calls where you drop in to chat with someone you like and who likes you. Those are called (5) _____ calls, not sales calls. They're usually unproductive but comforting.
(6) _____, you should be setting a sales call goal. (7) _____ _____, desired outcome, or intended result. Before making a sales call, ask yourself, "What do I want to accomplish or have happen as a result of this call?" (8) _____, perhaps you shouldn't be wasting your time or your prospect's time.

**Task Two:** You're going to hear five sentences. Repeat each sentence you hear. Then listen again and write down each sentence. Check your answer when you listen for the third time.

(1) _____
(2) _____
(3) _____

(4) _____

(5) _____

## ⓒ Conversations

**Conversation 1**

> *Task One:* Listen to the telephone conversation and choose the best answer.

(1) Who is Tony calling?
   A. A new client.               B. An old client.
   C. A telephone salesperson.    D. A competitor.

(2) What is the main purpose of Tony's call?
   A. To introduce new products.
   B. To make an after-sales maintenance call.
   C. To offer some discount.
   D. To update the company's contact information.

(3) The recent improvements are good because they _____.
   A. have successfully expanded their market share
   B. have no problem in operation
   C. give lower fuel efficiency and greater production costs
   D. give greater fuel efficiency and lower production costs

(4) From this conversation, we may learn that _____.
   A. their competitors don't have any updated version
   B. they don't have any updated version
   C. their competitors' market share has been falling in recent years
   D. their market share has been falling in recent years

(5) Which of the following is true?
   A. Some technical problems occurred in the engine the client has bought.
   B. The new engine is going to be offered free to the client.
   C. Tony will probably call again that day.
   D. The client is annoyed by the call.

> *Task Two:* Listen to the conversation again and rearrange the steps the phone-maker carries out in this conversation, by writing 1, 2, 3, etc. next to each step.

_____ State the purpose of his call: to tell more about the improvements to their products.

_____ Describe the new features of the engine.

_____ Make a comparison with the competitors' models.

    _____ Ask if the client is satisfied with the previous product they have bought.

    _____ Schedule for another call if this one is not convenient.

    _____ Explain how the new features will help to reduce production costs.

    _____ Explain the present market share situation.

    _____ Show some performance data of the engine's fuel efficiency.

**Conversation 2**

> ***Task One:*** Listen to the speaker's blog (containing a conversation in it), and discuss the cause of the failure of this call, then write down your answers on the lines below. Try to list as many as you can.

The following is the rest of the author's blog explaining why the call failed and providing some suggestions. Teachers may regard it as a reference.

(1) _____

(2) _____

(3) _____

(4) _____

(5) _____

(6) _____

> ***Task Two:*** Listen to the conversation again. Think of what effect the conversation on the left may produce. Match the conversation on the left with the writer's feelings on the right.

(1) Him: ... back then we talked about our search engine.

    Me: Okay, if you say so.

    A. Sighing and annoyed at such a dumb question.

(2) Him: Are you interested in new ways to market your business?

    Me: Of course.

    B. As if I were an idiot for not allowing him to make a pitch.

(3) Him: So, you aren't interested in new ways to market your business?

    Me: No, I guess not.

    C. Getting annoyed.

(4) Him: (acting incredulous) Okay then, have a good day.

    D. Amazed I haven't hung up yet.

**Right match:** (1) _____ ; (2) _____ ; (3) _____ ; (4) _____ .

## D Passage

> ***Task One:*** Listen to the passage and decide whether the following statements are true (T) or false (F).

(1) It is the boss who pays your salary and determines your company's future. ( )
(2) The best way to meet customer needs is to be a customer yourself. ( )
(3) Customers will evaluate principles, values and virtues of the salespeople. ( )
(4) According to the passage electronic commerce and marketing over the Internet are not yet mature. ( )
(5) Sales professionals must learn from the past, plan for the present and live in the future. ( )

*Task Two:* Listen to the passage again, and fill in the following chart with key words learned from the passage.

| Elements | Predictions |
| --- | --- |
| Customers | (1) Customers will drive business _____ in the future. <br> (2) Soft sell, _____ and relationship building with customers are the coming trends. <br> (3) Customers will demand _____, _____ and ethical responsibility from sales people. |
| Salespeople | (1) Do not work just for money, _____ or ego boost. <br> (2) Do work for _____. |
| Tools for business | _____ will become the most powerful marketing tool in history. |

# Part 4  Fun Listening

*Task One:* The word *pun* means the amusing use of a word or phrase that has two meanings. Listen to the recording and write down the puns. There is at least one pun in each question-and-answer pair. The pun in the first pair has been given to you.

(1) _____
(2) _____
(3) _____
(4) _____
(5) _____
(6) _____

**Task Two:** Listen to another poem *I wanna* and fill in the blanks with the words provided below.

| football table, | lunch, | view, | boss, | car, | three, | overpaid, |
| corner office, | free, | bonus, | underworked, | couch, | stocks, | ten |

**I Wanna**

I Wanna
I wanna be _____
and _____ .
I wanna daily _____
and _____ to trade.

I wanna start at _____
and leave at _____ .
I wanna four hour _____
and I want it for _____ .

I wanna _____
and an amazing _____ .
I wanna _____
and a _____ that's new.

I wanna be my own _____
and a _____ I can flaunt.
I wanna have more.
That's all I want.

214 | Unit 16  *How was the last order*

# Appendix

## 常用口语表达用语

### 1 Greetings

1. How are you?
2. How do you do?
3. How are you doing?
4. How's everything?
5. How's it going?
6. I've been looking forward to meeting you.
7. I have heard so much/a lot about you.
8. Glad/Nice to meet/see you!
9. Fancy meeting you here!
10. Long time no see.
11. You look great today.
12. Give me a hug.

### 2 Introduction

13. I would like to introduce myself. I'm...
14. Mary, let me introduce...
15. Allow me to introduce...
16. May I have your name?
17. John, may I introduce Mary to you?
18. I'd like you to meet Mary.
19. This is my friend John.
20. Can I have your business card?
21. Here is my business card.
22. Melinda, this is Roger. Roger, this is Melinda.
23. Sorry I didn't catch your name.

### 3 Farewells

24. See you (later).
25. See you soon.
26. See you tomorrow/next year!
27. So long.
28. Hope to see you again.
29. I am afraid that I must be leaving.
30. I am sorry but I have to go now.
31. I've got to go now.
32. Have a pleasant journey.
33. Have a good journey, and all the best.
34. Take care of yourself and don't forget to keep in touch.
35. I am looking forward to seeing you again.
36. Remember the good time we shared!

### 4 Thanks

37. Many thanks.
38. I'm much obliged to you.
39. Thanks a lot.
40. Thanks ever so much.
41. I can never thank you enough.
42. Thank you for all you've done for me.
43. Thanks for the trouble you have taken for me.
44. I appreciate your help.
45. I'm truly grateful for your help.
46. I couldn't have done it without you.
47. You saved my life.
48. You're one in a million.

### 5 Apologies

49. I'm really sorry.

50. I apologize for...
51. Please accept my heartfelt apology.
52. I beg your forgiveness.
53. I feel really bad/sorry about...
54. I'm really sorry for not keeping my promise.
55. I'm not sure how to put it, but I'm sorry that I have done something wrong to you.
56. It must have been very embarrassing to...
57. I'll never forgive myself.
58. Will you ever forgive me?
59. How could I be so thoughtless?
60. It's all my fault.
61. I didn't mean it.

## 6　Invitation

62. Would you like to join...?
63. I am wondering if you'd like to go to the...
64. I'll be happy if you can come to the...
65. I'd like to have dinner with you next Tuesday.
66. I wonder if you two would like to come to...
67. Let's go and have something.
68. We should be delighted if you could...
69. Would you be free to a concert on Sunday?
70. What about going to...?
71. Why not join...?
72. Why don't you come on a holiday with us?

## 7　Asking for Permission

73. Is it all right if I...?
74. Do you mind my doing...?
75. Would you mind my doing...?
76. Can I possibly have the book for a moment?
77. Do you have any objection to my doing...?
78. Am I allowed to make a suggestion?
79. Would I be in a position to express my opinion on this?
80. Would it be possible for me to put off the work till a later day?
81. I wonder whether I could take it away?
82. I'd like to make a phone call here, if you permit me.

## 8　Wishes and Congratulations

83. Wish you every success!
84. Good luck to you.
85. Wish you good luck (forever).
86. Wish you peace and happiness (during the holidays).
87. Let me wish you the best of everything.
88. May you succeed at whatever you try.
89. May all your wishes come true.
90. I wish you every fortune and every success.
91. May your Christmas be filled with joy and warmth!
92. Hope the holidays find you happy and healthy.
93. If only I had more time, I could do it.
94. Keep my fingers crossed that I'll win the first prize.
95. I'm sure you'll be happy together.
96. You make a great couple.
97. Congratulations! I knew you'd pass it with flying colors.
98. I want to congratulate you with all my heart.
99. I think no one deserves it more than you!
100. Please send him my congratulations.
101. What marvelous news!

## 9　Offering or Asking for Help

102. What can I do for you?
103. Is there anything I can do for you?
104. Let me help you with...
105. Let me give you a hand.
106. Don't worry. I'll do it for you.
107. Why don't you use my...?
108. I'll give you a lift if you like.
109. I'd like to help if I can.
110. Would you please...?
111. Could you do me a favor?

## 10　Making Appointments

112. What time is convenient for you?
113. What's the best place to meet?
114. What about Saturday evening?
115. Would tomorrow morning suit you?
116. May I expect you at five?
117. I'm wondering if you'd like to go to a movie with me.

118. I'm going to see the film with a group of my friends. Would you like to join us?
119. I'm afraid I won't be able to see you today.
120. I'm awfully sorry that I have to postpone my appointment with the dentist on Saturday.
121. Something urgent happened. I'd like to change our appointment to the day after tomorrow.
122. I really want to, but I have got hundreds of things to do.
123. Count me in if you are to meet on Sunday.
124. Glad you could make it.

## 11  Making Telephone Calls

125. May I speak to...?
126. Speaking.
127. Is Roger there?
128. Yes, speaking.
129. Hi, my hands are tied. I'll get back to you in a minute.
130. Can I call back? Something has come up.
131. Can I have your name and telephone number?
132. I have to take your number and call you back.
133. Can you connect me with...?
134. I'm afraid you've got the wrong number.
135. Can we continue this later? My other line is ringing.
136. Hang on a second/a moment.
137. Would you like to hold?
138. Hold the line, please.
139. He's not here right now.
140. He's in a meeting now.
141. He's out on his lunch break right now. Would you like to leave a message?
142. He's not available now. Can I take a message?
143. When he comes back, can you have him call me at 86-20-86345567?
144. May I leave a message?
145. Of course. Hold on for just a second so I can grab a pen and paper.
146. Can you put Daisy back on again? I forgot to tell her something.
147. Sure. I'll go and get her.
148. Long-distance call from...
149. Should I tell him you'll call back, or do you want him to call you?
150. If you leave your name and number, I'll have him call you back as soon as he's available.
151. Have you got the telephone directory? Can you help me get Mr. Li's telephone number?
152. John is on another line now. Can you hold on?

## 12  Having Meals

153. Could you show us the menu?
154. Would you like to see the menu?
155. Are you ready to order?
156. What do you recommend?
157. Which do you prefer?
158. How would you like that prepared/done?
159. What would you like to drink, tea or coffee?
160. I prefer noodles to rice.
161. I prefer to drink coffee without sugar.
162. What is your favorite...?
163. What about having western food today?
164. Let's grab something to eat!
165. It is very delicious, but I can't eat any more.
166. We will go Dutch.
167. Tonight's on me.
168. I'll take care of the bill/check.
169. Would I have the bill?
170. We'd like the bill, please.
171. Bring me the bill/check, please.

## 13  Seeing the Doctor

172. What's the matter?
173. What's the trouble with you?
174. What seems to be the trouble?
175. I don't feel like eating.
176. How long have you been like this?
177. I've been sick for a day.
178. It hurts me when I breathe.
179. I feel feverish.
180. I'd like to run some tests.
181. I'd like to take a blood sample.

182. Have you had this problem before?
183. How's your blood pressure?
184. Give up smoking and keep on taking more exercises.
185. I'm going to write a prescription.
186. What sort of medicine do you take?
187. Take the medicine, and you'll be better.
188. Take these pills every four hours.
189. He is up and about now.

## 14  Shopping

190. May/Can I help you?
191. Are you looking for something particular?
192. We have a clearance sale today.
193. The price will go down.
194. I heard other stores were having great mark—downs on this item.
195. Please try it on.
196. I've seen this cheaper in other places.
197. Could you bring the price down?
198. That is a steal.
199. I'd buy this if it were cheaper.
200. It's a little overpriced.
201. Do you know what size you wear?
202. I'm afraid we're out of that item.
203. I'm afraid we don't have it in stock.
204. Where is the men's shop?
205. Do you have this in stock?
206. Do you have this in blue?
207. How are you going to pay? Cash, check or charge?
208. How will you pay for this?
209. Cash back?
210. What a deal!
211. Bring your receipt to the customer service, and they will refund you.
212. Can you give me the invoice?

## 15  Asking the Way

213. Excuse me, can you tell me the way to...?
214. Could you tell me where I can find a hospital?
215. Sorry to trouble you, but can you direct me out of this building?
216. Which direction is it to...?
217. Excuse me, is this the right way to...?
218. Tell me, please, where is No. 27 on this street?
219. Excuse me, how can I get to...?
220. Excuse me, does this bus go to...?
221. How long does it take to walk there?
222. How can I find...?

## 16  Talking about Weather

223. Have you heard the weather forecast?
224. What does the weather forecast say?
225. We'll have fine weather for the next few days.
226. What will it be after the clear weather?
227. It says a storm may come soon.
228. How long will this hot weather last?
229. I hope it stays nice for the whole month.
230. It's wonderful after the rain.
231. Autumn is the best season here.
232. It's hot like oven now in this part of the country.
233. The weather is terribly changeable at this time of the year.
234. We don't know what's going to be tomorrow until we listen to the latest weather report.
235. It has turned out to be a nice day.
236. It seems to be clearing up.

## 17  Advice and Suggestions

237. If I were you, I'd phone him now.
238. What do you think I should do?
239. I advise you to see a doctor.
240. I would try again if I were you.
241. You'd better go through your test paper again.
242. Should we go now?
243. You ought to contact the police.
244. Why don't you go to bed earlier?
245. Don't you think it might be a good idea to have a picnic this weekend?
246. How about going to a concert?
247. I don't think it is very practical.

248. I recommend you to give up smoking.
249. May I suggest leaving a message with his secretary?
250. Isn't there anything else I could do?

## 18 Showing Attitude

251. It's cool! / Cool.
252. It is neat!
253. It is righteous!
254. That's great!
255. That's incredible!
256. The house is gorgeous!
257. You are brilliant/great/terrific/... !
258. It is a terrific game.
259. I am sick and tired of doing homework.
260. The movie was a turn-off.
261. You scared me!
262. That's so stupid!
263. It's a piece of cake.
264. No ifs, or buts.

## 19 Expressing Anger

265. What do you think you are doing?
266. I simply can't bear to see her behavior.
267. I'm very annoyed at...
268. I'm fed up with...
269. That's what gets me down.
270. I will not put up with...
271. It makes me sick the way he laughs/speaks...
272. You're getting on my nerves.
273. I've had enough of you.
274. Who do you think you are?
275. It makes me sick!
276. I've had enough of your...

## 20 Expressing Disappointment

277. I've expected it to be more exciting.
278. It wasn't as good as I'd expected.
279. Her performance could have been better.
280. I don't think much of the painting/story...
281. I was really looking forward to having a good time there.
282. That's a real letdown.
283. I must say I had hoped for twelve percent discount at least.
284. I must admit I had expected you to tell me the truth.
285. I wish I'd realized it.
286. The story wasn't up to much.
287. I've never felt so let down before.

## 21 Expressing Complaint

288. I want to make a complaint about...
289. What's the point of talking about it?
290. I've just had enough of that!
291. She is all talking.
292. Couldn't you speak a bit slowly/turn down the radio a little bit?
293. I wish you would come here earlier next time.
294. You should have seen the mess.

## 22 Expressing Sympathy

295. I'm sorry to hear about it.
296. You must be feeling bad/terrible/awful about...
297. Don't take it too much to heart.
298. Don't let it get you down.
299. It's no use crying over spilt milk.
300. It could have happened to anybody.
301. You can't win them all the time.
302. You must be annoyed about...
303. I am deeply sorry to learn/hear about...
304. I do hope it's nothing serious.
305. What bad luck!
306. Is there any way I can help?

## 23 Expressing Encouragement

307. Come on, be a man!
308. That's better than I can do.
309. I believe you can improve it.
310. I think you should go ahead.
311. If at first you don't succeed, try, try and try again.
312. You have my whole-hearted support.
313. There is no reason to feel discouraged.
314. The longest road must have an end.

315. Keep it up!
316. I'll be always there for you!

## 24 Making a Request

317. I was wondering whether you could...
318. May I trouble you to (do)...?
319. May I have the pleasure of ...?
320. Do you mind if I ...?
321. I'd appreciate it if you could help me with...
322. Do you think it would be possible to (do)...?
323. Would you be so kind as to...?
324. It would help me a great deal if you...
325. I'd be feeling grateful to you if you...

## 25 Expressing Surprise

326. My goodness!
327. That's incredible!
328. What a surprise!
329. I can't believe my eyes.
330. Wow! What a beautiful lake!
331. Good heavens!
332. How astonishing/amazing!
333. Who knows? God knows!
334. It's too good to be true!
335. Who could have thought/expected it!

## 26 Expressing Certainty or Uncertainty

336. Are you sure about...?
337. Is there any doubt about...?
338. I am sure about...
339. I am absolutely positive about...
340. I have no doubt about...
341. I'm quite convinced of...
342. There is little doubt in my mind about...
343. There is no question about...
344. I'm a hundred percent certain about...
345. I really can't tell about...
346. I have no idea about...
347. There is surely some doubt about...
348. It's not likely that...
349. It's hard to say.
350. It's obvious that ...
351. I'm certain/sure that...
352. I couldn't say for certain, but I suspect that ...

## 27 Agreeing and Disagreeing

353. Sure./Absolutely.
354. You got it.
355. By all means.
356. That's true/right.
357. That's for sure.
358. I couldn't agree with you more.
359. I don't think so.
360. That's not right.
361. I couldn't disagree with you more.
362. That's out of the question.
363. You've got it all wrong.
364. I don't think you've got your facts straight.
365. Next time get the facts first.
366. Don't jump to conclusions.